Memories

of the

Wensleydale

Railway

Tony Eaton

Copyright (Tony Eaton.)

ISBN 0-9536331-3-6

First published 2003
By ReCall Publications.

50,Turker Lane,
Northallerton.
North Yorkshire.
DL6 1QA
[01609] 774439

tony@eaton63.fsnet.co.uk

www. recallpublications.co.uk

Printed by
Thurston Printers, 6 Amber Street, Saltburn-by-the-Sea, Cleveland TS12 1DT
Telephone: (01287) 623756

www.thurstonprinters.co.uk

Introduction.

There have been several excellent and well researched books written about the Wensleydale Railway that have traced the origins of the line and the types of rolling stock and the many stations along its route, chiefly by Christine Hallas, Stanley Jenkins and C.D. Goode. This book differs greatly inasmuch that it is a pastiche of the myriad of stories about some of the hundreds of men and women who worked in the many and disparate trades and jobs on the line, with all the humour and drama that accompanies working on a small branch railway. There are stories about station masters, engine drivers, guards, signalmen, porters, motor drivers, clerks, track walkers and the almost forgotten gate keepers. Giving the stories more authenticity are scores of unpublished photographs both monochrome and colour. Included are rare photographs of a little known facet of the railway branch line, the horse box division when famous winners of classic races were delivered to and from the stables at Middleham and Richmond. Although most stories within the pages are of a humourous nature, it would not ring true if some of the more serious and sad events were not included. Therefore the accidents that occurred on the line with all the heartbreak that they brought, will hopefully convey to the reader that working on a railway has its inherent dangers as well as its mundane hours of toil and occasional pleasures.

Tony Eaton

Front Cover: A Diesel Stone Train coming out of Redmire (John Fitzgerald)

Dedication

I dedicate this book to the generations of men and women who worked on the Wensleydale Line and the generations of passengers who travelled from each and every one of that neat string of bucolic stations that once proudly bestrode the Northallerton to Garsdale railway. I also dedicate the book to those ageing stalwarts who are alive with memories of their years spent working on and maintaining that picturesque gem of a branch line that is held in such high affection by so many worldwide.

Other books by the author

From The Dales to Jericho. The Story of Alan Broadley. DSO DFC DFM Published 1997

Sunters-High Wide & Mighty. Published 2001

Two Friends-Two Different Hells. Published 2002

Acknowledgments

My gratitude and thanks go out to the following people both former employees and those who had reason to remember the Wensleydale line who so generously gave of their time, loaned precious photographs and documents with no time limit laid for their return.

FORMER EMPLOYEES.

Alyn Armstrong, Sue Appleby, Ken Appleby, Derick Appleton, Laurie Atkinson, James Blades, Ken Brown, Lanny Cass, Bill Catchpole, George Catchpole, Norman Darby, Jack Dent, Derek Fawcett, George Foster, Alan Gaythorpe, Kathleen Gaythorpe, Harry Hartley, Alan Hiscock, Sheila Houseman, Wilf Houseman, Irving, Ursula Jackson, Dick Pashby [Snr] Dick Pashby [Jr] Artie Rainbow, Fred Stevens, Mr. Stannard, Eric Walker, Maurice Weighell.

ASSOCIATED PARTIES.

Prudence Carlton, Peter Blakey, Elizabeth Bradley, Lou Dale, Edgar Daykin, Pat Dent, Mrs. Dinsdale, Barry Foster, Mr. Gill, Jack Horner, Alan and David Jobling, Mr&Mrs Megginson, Colin Narramore, Charles Parker, Anne Pashby, Tom Pearson, Brian Redhead, Olive Robinson, Jim Sedgewick, David Severs, Maurice Simpson, Eva Shuttleworth, Colin Walls, Constance Walls, Mr.&Mrs. Wilkinson, Philip Yardley.
Research sources.

The Public Record Office, The Northallerton Archive, North Yorkshire County Library, The Northern Echo, Darlington & Stockton Times, Darlington Library, The Railway Weighells, A special acknowledgement to Stanley Jenkins and Christine Hallas for their respective books, The Wensleydale Branch and The Wensleydale Railway respectively. The Wensleydale Railway Association and John King via the Ian Bell collection, the Jim Sedgewick collection.

SPECIALIST SERVICES

Illustrations by Neil Wooding. [N.A.P.A.] Book cover Graphics by Sean Statters. Brian Redhead, Journalist.

PROOF READERS AND EDITORS.

Jack Bosomworth, Ken Wilson, Gill Dixon and Michael Bentley.
Peter Blakey for advancing the idea for the writing of the book.

My thanks and acknowledgments to all donors of photographs and documents are recorded on this page and not by each individual illustration.

Tony Eaton.
Northallerton. May 2003.

Contents

The Line from East to West

Northallerton, the County Town and Headquarters of North Yorkshire is rich in the history of the railway network that courses unerringly through the eastern reaches of the country. The main line from London's King's Cross to Edinburgh's Waverly Station, spears its way through or past many of the towns and villages of rural North Yorkshire and Northallerton is one of the many stopping points on its way. In what was known as the golden age of steam, such illustrious locomotives as The Flying Scotsman and Sir Nigel Gresley and scores of other smoking express trains thundered their irrepressible way both to the north and south of Britain. In the long and spectacular history of rail travel, village after village adjacent to the main line of North Yorkshire had the distinction of having a railway station as almost part and parcel of village life, and next to agriculture, was for many the main provider of employment. Otterington, Newby Wiske, Danby Wiske, East Cowton, to name but a few of those villages that heard and witnessed those smoking steaming firebrands as they passed by their homes, each one boasting a population numbered in the low hundreds. The larger town of Thirsk seven miles south of Northallerton also enjoyed visits of those locomotives and was an important rail junction in its own right. Today the streamlined diesel/electric locomotives in the livery of Virgin and GNER swish by those very same villages at speeds in excess of 100 mph, intermingled with the more sedate carriages of Arriva and Connex commuter trains that bustle in and through the stations from Tees-side en route to the western reaches of the country.

The reality of having a railway station on one's doorstep was a source of pride to the inhabitants of those bucolic villages and great care and time was taken in keeping the stations as spick and span as could be achieved. Not only were there mainline express trains passing north and south through those stations, there was until recent times, a local service that headed west from Northallerton through to Garsdale, known as the Wensleydale Branch.

Before the advent of the motor car and the omnibus this line was for many people in those lonely districts the only form of travel readily available and until the laying of the mainline from London to Darlington in 1841, the population of this part in the Yorkshire Dales was virtually immobile, save for the very wealthy who could afford to travel by stagecoach or private horse drawn vehicle. With the completion of the Gateshead stretch of the main line railway in 1844, the industrial vitality of the region began to stir as freight and passenger services became the lifeline of the community. Although many of the smaller stations on the main line were not stopping places for the mainline trains, the market town of Northallerton was designated to be a station where trains would halt and where a ticket for an express could be purchased. With the opening of the main line to Northallerton, impetus for trade to the Yorkshire Dales increased with the building of the Northallerton-Hawes Branch Railway, which was completed by 1877. Although many aspects of trade and commerce had been ongoing in the Dales for many years, it was the advent of the laying of that branch rail line that led to industrial quarrying in Wensleydale. The pulling power of the steam engine had made the carrying of large quantities of limestone to Dorman and Long steel works and later British Steel/CORUS a viable proposition. In 1854, the Stockton Branch Railway built and opened a goods station at the North End of the town. Engine sheds and a series of signal boxes were built close to the main line, resulting in Northallerton becoming an important railway town in its own right, albeit a small one.

The Wensleydale line heading west from Northallerton, had many station stopping points and crossing gates on its somewhat tortuous and hilly journey through the Yorkshire Dales. Almost all small towns and villages en route had a charming station and platform replete with all that was necessary for the running of a passenger/freight rail service to say nothing of an abundance of floral display. The stations situated along the route from Northallerton to Hawes were;
Northallerton, Ainderby, Scruton, Leeming Bar, Bedale, Crakehall, Jervaulx [Newton le Willows]* Finghall Lane, Constable Burton, Spennithorne, Harmby Quarry, Leyburn, Wensley, Redmire, Aysgarth, Askrigg, and Hawes. There were also several manned gate crossings on the route.
Some time later a final stretch of line was linked from Hawes Junction to Garsdale which was part of the LMS line.
That number of stations en route made the entire rail journey from Northallerton to Garsdale a distance of 39 3/4 miles. However in the rush of enthusiasm to build the line, no great study was made of the long term financial viability of the project. [In the event it was found to be less profitable than at first envisaged] *In reality Jervaulx station was at the village of Newton le Willows but the change of name was to prevent confusion with the town of Newton le Willows in Lancashire.*

The scheduling of the passengers trains led to some peculiar and somewhat plodding journey times between Northallerton and Garsdale, the two distant termini. There follows a small sample of those schedules. In 1875 there were four return trains scheduled between Northallerton and Leyburn and one between Northallerton and Bedale, all worked by the resident Leyburn engine. The first running at 6.am and arriving at 9.30 pm, with the journey time varying between 55 and 65 minutes. In 1904 there was a scheduled 4.am mail train to Hawes that apparently 'metamorphosed' into an unlikely express for the return trip, by the simple expedient of realigning the lamps on the front and the rear of the train. As an express, it left at 9.15 am and took a 'mere' one hour and 14 minutes to travel to Northallerton, and strictly speaking that was expressive speed. Sometime later the scheduled 6.32am train from Northallerton took an excruciating 173 minutes to reach Hawes junction. In all fairness to the schedulers, it was booked to 'stand' at Hawes for sixty minutes but yet, was classed as a 'through' train! Generally speaking the passenger service along the line was without doubt, a slow one. Something in the order of two hours was the usual running time for the whole journey but often it took longer due to weather and other unforeseen problems.

Jim 'Pinky' Blades of Hawes, who joined the line after the war, recalls the slowness of the service when catching the Hawes train from Northallerton whilst on leave from the navy. He says with a smile and a shrug of resignation that no sooner had the train got up a 'head of steam' it would then begin its braking sequence to run into the next station en route, so making the journey a series of puffs, chuffs and squealing brakes. Sometimes the engine would almost run out of breath as it encountered some of the gradients in the Dales which might have also coincided with the fireman not keeping up a sufficient head of steam for the engine to conquer the climbs [An altitude of 750ft above sea-level had to be reached]. However these problems were reversed on the return leg as it was almost a case of almost free-wheeling down the gradients. In the early days limestone trains were so heavily laden travelling from Redmire, that messages were sent ahead to the signalmen en route with a request to have the gates open well in advance to allow the trains to pass. The reason? The braking systems could not cope with the weight of the fully laden moving trains on a downward gradient. Later, braking tenders were coupled to the engines of the ore trains which gave greater braking resistance allowing them to stop within a reasonable distance. However the problems of gradients weren't unique to Wensleydale, all railway routes with a multitude of villages and built in natural climbs suffered similar problems.

The passenger service on the line never did come up to expectations as the Dales area that it served was sparsely populated. The two largest towns that it served were, Leyburn which had a population of 6,000 and Northallerton with 5,000 plus and several smaller towns/villages of only a few hundred people and farmsteads were the limits of its catchments area potential. Freight traffic was by far the greater source of income for the line but eventually that was not able to sustain its viability. Schools used it for the transportation of pupils from the various villages to and from Northallerton and from the upper reaches of Aysgarth and Hawes, but an inevitability of decline settled on the line and that decline accelerated with the advent of regular bus services and the availability of the motor car. Fare prices were also a factor. The rail fare to any of the villages on the line was almost double that of the bus, and the train generally took longer to arrive at its destinations. There was one upsurge in passenger traffic in 1927 when on the 29th of June of that year, eight 'eclipse' specials steamed into Leyburn and Aysgarth full of 'eclipse watchers' arriving from all parts of the country. This phalanx of specials was accompanied by two catering trains complete with kitchen cars and two 3rd class open carriages to provide refreshments. As successful as that day might have been, there was never again to be anything like that number of passengers to use the line on any given day save for its valedictory closure run. The line enjoyed a brief upsurge in passenger and freight traffic during the Second World War, but the arrival of peace brought that burgeoning prosperity to an end. On Saturday the 24th of April 1954 the last official passenger train meandered its way to Hawes and returned. On the 26th the service officially ceased running. Although British Railways closed down the passenger service, the freight and parcels service was allowed to operate until 1964 when that too was stopped. Redmire and Leyburn stations were given a stay of closure due to the leading of stone from Redmire, as was Jervaulx for the transporting of scholars from Aysgarth School. The effect of the closures signalled the end of a much loved but rarely used railway branch line. Mineral traffic from Redmire kept it operating for a number of years and then the Ministry of Defence paid for vital maintenance of the track for the use of transporting of tanks and armoured cars, and today that is all that plies this erstwhile steamy and smoking branch line, be it very rarely.

A timetable for the Wensleydale line showing evidence of the leisurely pace of travel.

Table 41

NORTHALLERTON, LEYBURN, HAWES and GARSDALE

Miles			WEEKDAYS											SUNDAYS	
			SO am	SX am	SX am	SO am	SO pm	SX pm	pm	pm	pm	pm		pm	
—	2 York	dep	3 50	3 50	8 35	8 35	12 10	..	..	3f 7	8 0	....		12 20	.. ..
—	2 Newcastle	dep	2 34	2 34	6 54	6 54	11a15	..	..	2 35	7 25	..		12 50	.. .. ..
—	2 Darlington	„	6 27	6 27	8 15	8 15	12 19	..	..	3 38	8 27	..		1 55	.. .. ..
—	NORTHALLERTON	dep	7 5	7 15	9 30	9 27	1 30	..	..	4 10	9 5	..		4 0	.. .. ..
3	Ainderby	„	7 13	7 23	....	....	....			4 18	9 13			....	
4¼	Scruton	„	7 17	7 27						4 22					
5¼	Leeming Bar	„	7 22	7 32	9 46	9 43	1 46			4 26	9 21			4 17	
7¼	Bedale	„	7 30	7 40	9 52	9 49	1 52			4 33	9 29			4 22	
9¼	Crakehall	„	7 36	7 46	9 58	9 55	1 58			4 38	9 35				
11¼	Jervaulx	„	7 44	7 54	10 2	9 59	2 6			4 42	9 39			4 32	
13¼	Finghall Lane	„	7 48	7 58	10 6	10 3	2 13			4 47	9 43			4 40	
14¼	Constable Burton	„	7 52	8 2	10 10	10 7	2 17			4 52	9 47				
15¾	Spennithorne	„	D	D	D	D	D			D	D			4 47	
17¾	Leyburn {	arr	8 1	8 11	10 19	10 16	2 26			5 1	9 55			4 47	
		dep	8 17	8 17		10 22	2 30	2 30		5 6					
20	Wensley	„	8 23	8 23		10 28	2 35	2 35		5 11	..			..	
22	Redmire	„	8 29	8 29		10 34	2 40	2 40		5 16					
25	Aysgarth	„	8 36	8 36		10 41	2 47	2 47		5 23					
29¾	Askrigg	„	8 45	8 45		10 50	2 56	2 56		5 32					
34	HAWES {	arr	8 54	8 54		10 59	3 5	3 5		5 41					
		dep	8 56	8 56		11 5			4 25	5 42					
39¾	GARSDALE	arr	9 10	9 10		11 19			4 39	5 56					
91	Carlisle	arr	10 46	10 40	....	2p12	....		....	7 30	....			....	

Miles			WEEKDAYS								SUNDAYS	
			SO am	SX am	SX am	SO am	SO pm	pm	pm	pm	pm	
—	Carlisle	dep	....	....	....	....	10a23	....	....	4 35		
—	GARSDALE	dep	..	..	10 41	10 47	12 55	3 16	..	6 40	..	..
5¼	HAWES {	arr	..	..	10 53	10 59	1 7	3 27		6 51		
		dep	..	..	10 56	11 2	1 9		4 0	6 53		
10	Askrigg	„	..	..	11 4	11 10	1 18		4 8	7 1		
14¼	Aysgarth	„	..	..	11 13	11 19	1 27		4 17	7 10		
17¾	Redmire	„	..	..	11 20	11 26	1 34		4 23	7 16		
19¾	Wensley	„	..	..	11 25	11 31	1 39		4 28	7 22		
22¼	Leyburn {	arr	....	....	11 30	11 36	1 44		4 33	7 27		
		dep	7 25	7 35	11 36	11 42	1 50		4 38	7 33	5 10	
24	Spennithorne	„	7 30	7 40					B	7 40	5 17	
25¼	Constable Burton	„	7 34	7 44	11 43	11 49	1 57		4 58	7 43	5 23	
26¼	Finghall Lane	„	7 37	7 47	11 46	11 52	2 0		5 2	7 47		
28¼	Jervaulx	„	7 42	7 52	11 50	11 56	2 7		5 6			
30	Crakehall	„	7 46	7 56	11 54	12 0	2 11		5 13	7 56	5 32	
32¼	Bedale	„	7 52	8 2	12 0	12 6	2 17		5 23	8 2	5 38	
34	Leeming Bar	„	7 58	8 8	12 6	12 12	2 23		5 27	BSO6		
35¼	Scruton	„	8 2	8 12						8 9		
36¼	Ainderby	„	8 6	8 16	12 14	12 20				8 9		
39¾	NORTHALLERTON	arr	8 13	8 23	12 21	12 27	2 40		5 40	8 16	5 53	
53¾	2 Darlington	arr	9 45	9 45	12 42	....	3 19		6 9	9 1	7 14	
90¼	2 Newcastle	„	10 49	10 49	1 38	..	4 19		7b17	9 52	8 23	
69¾	2 York	arr	9g20	9 20	1 26	1 26	4 44	....	7 0	9h13	6 52	

B—Calls when required to set down.
D—Calls when required to set down from Northallerton.
SO—Saturdays only.
SX—Saturdays excepted.
a—am.

b—On Fridays commencing 19th June, Mondays commencing 13th July and on Saturdays arrives Newcastle 7.12 pm.
f—On Saturdays departs York 2.25 pm.

g—From 20th June to 12th September inclusive arrives York 9.1 am.
h—On Fridays 24th July to 21st August arrives York 8.58 pm.
p—pm.

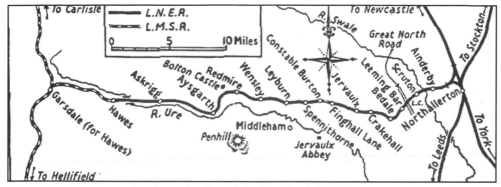

A schematic plan of the Wensleydale Railway.

That stretch of railway in the Yorkshire Dales provided employment for many hundreds of people over the nine decades of its existence until final closure in the 1960s. This book tells the stories of some of the many men and women who 'Worked the Wensleydale Line' and of those who travelled and experienced the vagaries and joys of patronising a small branch railway. Even in modern times railways by definition are labour intensive and the requirements and skills of each and every member of staff are vital to the efficient running of the line. In the heyday of the Wensleydale line, the numbers of men and women employed to keep it running was quite considerable with small village stations employing several porters, clerks, signalmen and of course the 'Master'. As vital as all support staff are, it is the engine driver that captures the imagination of the public and 'wanting to be an engine driver' can still be the dream of many small boys, although with the demise of the steam loco, the dream is not quite so vivid. There were many characters on the engine footplates and they figure largely in the story of the 'Line'. Apart from the men who crewed the trains, the driver, his fireman and the guard, there was a host of other workers who were an integral part in the running and maintenance of the railway and management of the stations. Rarely seen office bound clerks and ubiquitous porters patrolling the platforms were supported by a host of engine shed workers, shunters, guards, platelayers and signalmen. Then ultimately there was the boss, the Station Master. It is with the 'Masters' that this story begins.

On a working railway of old, the pinnacle position of all station staff that had 'hands on' control is, or was the Station Master. Sadly that exalted position has disappeared along with a host of other time honoured traditions and customs. The very name Station Master has an unequivocal ring about it and tells one and all that he is the boss and he is the one who gives the orders. The Wensleydale Railway has had many station masters in its long and distinguished history and one of the longest serving was Tom Plummer, the 'Master' of Bedale station.

The Station Master

Tom Plummer of Bedale

Tom Plummer was born in 1902 near Leeds and was the son of the station master at Constable Burton. Tom started work as a junior clerk in 1916 along side his father at Constable Burton and from there he worked in various clerical grades, at such places as, Northallerton, Knaresborough, Catterick, Barnard Castle, Brotton and Ormesby. In 1943 he became 'Master' of Bedale station and was to remain there for the next twenty three years. When Tom arrived at Bedale the number of staff working there was very impressive. There were two signalmen, two porters, four drivers and half a dozen clerks. Among the members of staff were his wife Elizabeth, who helped with the sale of coal, [a perk for the station master in those days] and his sister in law Miss Alice Horn. Tom and Elizabeth met while they were both working as clerks at Redmire station. They married in 1928 with Alice acting as chief bridesmaid.

Not only did Tom Plummer run the station efficiently as a railway establishment, he ensured that it looked pleasing to the eye and at all times it was kept clean and tidy. Floral displays with plants grown in a greenhouse by Elizabeth and Alice adorned the approaches of the station and the well swept platform. In regional competitions organised by British Rail in 1953, Bedale won two first prizes for best gardens and best kept station, and in the summer of 1949 a second prize. During the Bedale pageant of 1951, Tom donned the classic attire of the station master, top hat and frock coat for the occasion. Suitably attired in full fig, he officially welcomed the first train of the pageant as if it were the first train that had arrived at the station a century earlier.

It was at this time that there was an official inspection of the stations on the branch by Mr. Charles Corps, the District Commercial Manager from Middlesbrough and from Darlington Ian McGregor, the District Operating Superintendent. Ken Appleby who was acting as holiday relief Station Master recalls a snippet of conversation between Tom Plummer and Mr. Corps. It went something like this;
"Plummer, you have been here far too long, why don't you apply for promotion to a higher grade station?" In his well known gentle and patient tones, Tom Plummer replied *"I would need a job as good as yours Mr. Corps before I would consider moving"* The

conversation then stopped and according to Ken Appleby the idea went down like a lead balloon.

Tom retired in 1966 after a career spanning fifty years. He had witnessed changes and events from wartime railways [WW1] the general strike, the boom in wartime traffic [WW11], the withdrawal of the passenger service, reduction in goods services, a visit by Her Majesty The Queen, and the Queen Mother, a resurgence of freight limestone to the final closure. When he finally left the railway he bought the station house that in which he and his wife had lived for many years, as his retirement home, where he Elizabeth and Alice lived the quiet life.

He kept himself busy with his gardening and greenhouse and playing bowls for the Bowling Green Society and amateur photography. He was also a member of the Beresford-Peirse Masonic Lodge at Bedale and the Probus 25 Club and all three, Tom, Elizabeth and Alice were members of Aiskew Methodist Church. In his retirement he was still involved in the railway albeit involuntarily when the Royal Train under heavy guard was parked within yards of his house while Prince Philip or Prince Charles went about their royal duties.

Tom Plummer died in 1997 aged 95. The industry of railways had lost a man who had served with distinction and dedication for fifty years and who was a respected member of the local community. During his long career he had served with the North Eastern Railway, the London and North Eastern and British Railways. It is fair to say that the likes of Tom Plummer will never be seen again.

A long view of Bedale platform and the level crossing.

*Tom Plummer
with a group
of Bedale staff.
Bill Dunn, Tom,
Harry Appleby,
Rail official, Alice Horn,
Tom's sister-in-law,
Herbert Jobling, ???
Frank Atkinson.*

*The award of RoSPA
Safe Driving Awards
Tom Plummer,
Mr. Hickman,
'Bumper' Harrison,
Herbert Jobling, ???
Rail official.*

With the final closure, local resident Tom Pearson, acquired the clock that once hung in Bedale station office. It was given to him gratis as it was in bits and pieces, rusting and covered with mud. Tom collected the remains and put them into a dustbin lid and took them home. Despite passing advice that he would never be able to 'get that thing going again' he did get it going again and it now takes pride of place in his collection of memorabilia and is also an excellent time keeper.

*Army RTO [Railway Transport Officers]
at Bedale station 1944
Captain Parker is in the centre.*

16

Charles Yardley of Leeming Bar.

Charles Yardley was the Station Master at Leeming Bar and until his retirement was another of the old guard railwaymen who like Tom Plummer accrued vast experience while working on different lines during his working life. Charles was born in 1903 at Carlton near the village Snaith on the outskirts of Selby and was the son of a stationmaster. He started work immediately after leaving school on the Hull Barnsley Railway. When that railway was absorbed into the North Eastern Railway he moved to the north east of England and worked as the booking office clerk at Newcastle. He eventually moved to the Northallerton area and during the war worked at Ainderby Steeple and then for a short time at Bolden Colliery before finally moving to Leeming Bar to take over as station master from Billy Hill. For a branch line station, Leeming Bar was well endowed with facilities. It boasted two platforms, a large signal box, busy sidings and coal yards and an elegant white portico on entering the station buildings. From the time the station opened it was without doubt the busiest station on the entire line not only for the normal goods traffic but for the business of a local brewery owned by Plews. Supplies of barley were often delivered and many hundreds of barrels of ale departed from the station during the brewing days. In 1925 Plews sold the business to Cameron's Breweries of Hartlepool. Cameron's promptly put the building up for sale which in turn was purchased by the Ryder Brothers [butchers] of Northallerton. Ryders opened the factory under the name of the Vale of Mowbray Company colloquially known as the 'Vom', complete with a towering chimney stack that became a visible landmark which could be seen for many miles distant. The factory produced among many things, bacon, pork pies and sausages by the wagon load and scores were transported weekly by rail to all parts of the country, including a small weekly parcel of half a dozen pies destined for Nairn in Scotland. [A wagon load of oak sawdust from York was shunted into the sidings for the smoking of the bacon] The air base RAF Leeming had many wagon loads of stores delivered to the sidings of the station and the local agriculture merchant, John Henry Gill utilised the same sidings for delivery of a whole variety of farming implements.

On his retirement Charles Yardley kept up his keen interest in gardening and amateur photography and his membership of the Beresford-Peirse Lodge of Freemasons. In his latter years Charles lived with his son Philip at Leyburn. He died in 1988 aged 85.

SPOTLIGHT

LEEMING BAR

LEEMING BAR would be regarded as an ordinary country station were it not for the unusual mixture of traffic which it handles. Situated on the Hawes branch, 5¾ miles from Northallerton and 34 from Garsdale (both recent "Spotlight" subjects), it is right in the heart of the Vale of Mowbray.

Leeming aerodrome is nearby and parts and accessories for planes are usual everyday traffic.

The Vale of Mowbray Bacon Factory sends out sufficient bacon each Monday to make rations for 3,000 people. In addition, LEEMING BAR handles a vast number of cartons of meat pies, sausage, and other off-the-ration food from the Vale of Mowbray factory, in addition to sorting and routing the contents of four van-loads of similar traffic weekly.

As though the assortment were not already sufficiently notable, LEEMING BAR station sends away a large number of agricultural implements loaded on special wagons from a local manufacturer.

To ensure that the station staff have few idle moments nurserymen in the vicinity offer boxes of cut blooms throughout the season and they are forwarded to Newcastle, Darlington and Leeds markets.

Passenger or freight traffic—it all comes the same to LEEMING BAR staff, who work together to keep the wheels turning.

Members of this team shown in our photographic strip are (top to bottom): Station Master C. W. Yardley, Station Clerk Joyce Merryweather, Porter Signalman Harold Gaythorpe, Clerk Ann Fowler and Porter Signalman William E. Archer.

Leeming Bar and staff as featured in 'Spotlight' the British Railways magazine in 1952. Featured are, Station Master Yardley, Ann Stubbs [nee Fowler], Harold Gaythorpe, Joyce Merryweather, Bill Archer

A view of the interior of Leeming Bar signal cabin.
The building seen through the window is the VOM pie factory,
now no longer standing due to a devastating fire in 2002.

Charles Yardley standing outside the portico at Leeming Bar station.
Note the poster on the wall informing the public of the cessation of passenger services.

Norman Darby of Leyburn

 Norman Darby first joined the railway in 1936 at Ilkley in West Yorkshire. The war interrupted his railway work as he was drafted into the RAF until 1945. After leaving the services he qualified as station master and his first post was at the very Welsh sounding but very much Yorkshire station of Ben Rhydding in the heart of the West Riding. After a short spell and having his position at Ben Rhydding usurped by a wartime served senior station master in 1959, Norman arrived at Leyburn. He and his wife took over the station master's house at Leyburn which by their usual standards was extremely large and extremely difficult to keep heated. The master bedroom [which used to be the board room for the meeting of rail officials] had four large windows which kept the temperature down somewhat.

He immediately set about making that very industrious and busy station a paying concern. His office staff at the time of his arrival were; Mr. Harry Pearson chief clerk, Sheila Houseman goods clerk and Elizabeth Allison horsebox clerk. Within a year of his arrival the horsebox business broke even after many years of making a loss and subsequently made a profit until the service was withdrawn in 1965. [See chapter *The Wensleydale Motor Driver*]

While Norman was in charge at Leyburn the Ministry of Defence reopened Bellerby army training camp on Bellerby moor and the sight and sounds of troop trains running through Leyburn station became a familiar feature of railway life with lines of light armoured cars being taken up to the camp for exercises. On one occasion when the Scots Guards had completed their stint of training at Bellerby, their military band played a farewell medley to Norman and his staff in appreciation for all the hard work that they had put in. Although things went well for Norman there were the occasional problems to overcome. At one part of the track there was regular derailing of engines with one particular awkward derailing at Wensley. In Norman's report he wrote a glowing tribute to the engineering staff and said that the job of re-railing the engine was 'expeditiously done' Another time an engine became derailed under a bridge at the station which once again tested the skills and the patience of the engineering recovery staff.

A study in concerned manpower.
The derailed loco at Wensley that caused great delay.

Norman's tenure at Leyburn coincided with the particularly severe winter of 1961-62 when shortly after the Christmas holiday period, heavy snowfalls were recorded all over the country and especially in the Yorkshire Dales. The Dales has always experienced harsh winters in terms of snow and frosts, but the winter 1961-62 was as severe as the winter of 1947 and tested the mettle of both the Dales folk and the people who worked in that part of the county. The snow lay up to one foot in depth and drifted to a height of fifteen feet completely cutting off whole communities. Travel by road was impossible and the bus service to the area was curtailed and there was no means of people being able to move around. Representations were made to British Railways for them to restore the passenger service to allow people to travel. This was agreed and for the first time since 1954 fare paying passengers were travelling from Northallerton to Hawes–The Wensleydale Line. There follows a draft of the report in the Darlington & Stockton Times on the reintroduction of the passenger service on January 6th 1962

The Darlington & Stockton Times. January 1962.
The snow blizzard on Saturday night brought chaos to Wensleydale. It left a foot of snow in the valleys and up to fifteen feet drifts blocking several main roads. Motor vehicles were abandoned in many parts of the Dale particularly on the Wensley to Redmire and Redmire to Carperby roads. On the Bainbridge to Hawes road the snow at Cupples Hill west of Bainbridge drifted up to a depth of several feet. Three milk lorries were abandoned on Saturday but were dug out by Sunday night.

The villages of Redmire and Carperby were isolated. The road was reopened through to Redmire by Sunday evening, but Carperby was not opened until Tuesday.

Several farms were isolated including Thoresby where Mr. Robert Foster accumulated four days milk supply using up all his containers. Milk churns were in short supply. On the Monday Councillor John Sunter, Chairman of Aysgarth Rural District Council, approached the Station Master at Leyburn, Mr. Norman Darby seeking his help with a passenger service. This was granted and a snow plough preceding the passenger train left Northallerton. After having difficulty at Leeming Bar due to frozen gates it came to Leyburn and on to Hawes where it encountered deep drifts opposite Cams House Farm. After its return the passenger train left Leyburn with nine passengers. It stopped at four closed stations en route, Wensley, Redmire, Aysgarth and Askrigg. At Aysgarth a further sixteen passengers entrained, of which thirteen were from the Willoughby County School in Hull.

Norman Darby with members of his staff standing next to the emergency passenger train laid on by British Rail in January 1962.

On the return journey down Wensleydale, the train stopped at stations and also opposite Thoresby Farm where Marmaduke Foster and two farm men had brought 22 milk churns. Another train ran from Leyburn to Hawes returning in the evening. At Hawes on the Tuesday there was an important   livestock mart sale which was able to take place due to the efforts of all railway staff.

Mr. Foster thanked the railway authorities for the concessions in providing a passenger service in the emergency. The fare charged for passengers was 7s.3d (36p) and the train with a form of heating came to be known as the 'Farmer's Express'

After the weather settled and things got back to normal, there were high hopes that British Railways might have reintroduced a limited passenger service on the line for the future. Sadly, the emergency service provided in January 1962 did not lead to the resumption of a permanent service between Northallerton and Hawes and things went back to 'normal'.

Much of the credit must go to Norman Darby and his staff for the sheer hard work and time that they all put in to make the passenger service work smoothly for its timely but limited availability. Norman was a public spirited man and believed strongly in working with the local authorities whenever help was required. Shortly after arriving at Leyburn he offered his services to the local constabulary to act as a Special Constable. He in fact was carrying on the role that he had undertaken while at Ben Rhydding. As the stationmaster there he was a special constable but his passenger guard was a sergeant. So when on railway duty, Norman was the boss but while on policing duty, his passenger guard was the boss. This was always a source of amusement to both of them.

As was the normal practice of Station Masters in the region, Norman had a franchise to sell coal to the local community. [Apparently the LNER was the only region to allow this] To his regret and annoyance, his sales were not in the least bit profitable. The siding where he kept his stock of coal backed onto open land and the coal had the habit of disappearing of a night time. Norman never did find out who the miscreants were, but he is certain that many a farmer had a bright and cheery living room fire during some harsh Dales winters. Very soon after a particularly heavy loss of coal, he closed down his entire business.

In early 1963 Her Majesty The Queen visited the local area and the Royal Train was to be parked between Leeming Bar and Bedale. However there was a strong possibility that the train might travel along the length of line to Leyburn. Even though it was only the faintest possibility, the rail authorities decided that all stations on the route would have to

Presentation of the St. John Ambulance Long Service Medal to Morley Ward with a horsebox as back drop. L to R Tom Metcalfe, Harry Jones, Elizabeth Clark, Sheila Houseman, Norman Darby, Morley Ward, Mr. Pearson, Mr. Lewis [BR].

have a coat of paint applied, but only on the part that Her ▓▓▓
the front.

At the end of 1963, Norman Darby left Leyburn ▓▓▓
promotion to Assistant Yard Master at Darlington. After a c▓▓▓
moved on to Middlesbrough as Assistant Divisional Manage▓▓▓
as Assistant Divisional Manager at Newcastle. Norman has ▓▓▓
the 'Dales' railway and would not have missed it for anyth i ▓▓▓
live in retirement in Darlington.

*The presentation of RoSPA safe driving
awards at Leyburn. Harry Pearson,
Tom Metcalfe, Harry Jones,
Mr. Lewis, Norman, Mike Heseltine.*

*Norman presenting a wallet full of
bank notes donated by the staff and
local people on the retirement of
signalman Nessfield Hartley.*

have a coat of paint applied, but only on the part that Her Majesty might actually see i.e. the front.

At the end of 1963, Norman Darby left Leyburn and the Wensleydale line on promotion to Assistant Yard Master at Darlington. After a couple of years at Darlington he moved on to Middlesbrough as Assistant Divisional Manager and ended his railway career as Assistant Divisional Manager at Newcastle. Norman has fond memories of his time on the 'Dales' railway and would not have missed it for anything. He and his wife Margaret live in retirement in Darlington.

The presentation of RoSPA safe driving awards at Leyburn. Harry Pearson, Tom Metcalfe, Harry Jones, Mr. Lewis, Norman, Mike Heseltine.

Norman presenting a wallet full of bank notes donated by the staff and local people on the retirement of signalman Nessfield Hartley.

to 'normal'.

Much of the credit must go to Norman Darby and his staff for the sheer hard work and time that they all put in to make the passenger service work smoothly for its timely but limited availability. Norman was a public spirited man and believed strongly in working with the local authorities whenever help was required. Shortly after arriving at Leyburn he offered his services to the local constabulary to act as a Special Constable. He in fact was carrying on the role that he had undertaken while at Ben Rhydding. As the stationmaster there he was a special constable but his passenger guard was a sergeant. So when on railway duty, Norman was the boss but while on policing duty, his passenger guard was the boss. This was always a source of amusement to both of them.

As was the normal practice of Station Masters in the region, Norman had a franchise to sell coal to the local community. [Apparently the LNER was the only region to allow this] To his regret and annoyance, his sales were not in the least bit profitable. The siding where he kept his stock of coal backed onto open land and the coal had the habit of disappearing of a night time. Norman never did find out who the miscreants were, but he is certain that many a farmer had a bright and cheery living room fire during some harsh Dales winters. Very soon after a particularly heavy loss of coal, he closed down his entire business.

In early 1963 Her Majesty The Queen visited the local area and the Royal Train was to be parked between Leeming Bar and Bedale. However there was a strong possibility that the train might travel along the length of line to Leyburn. Even though it was only the faintest possibility, the rail authorities decided that all stations on the route would have to

Presentation of the St. John Ambulance Long Service Medal to Morley Ward with a horsebox as back drop. L to R Tom Metcalfe, Harry Jones, Elizabeth Clark, Sheila Houseman, Norman Darby, Morley Ward, Mr. Pearson, Mr. Lewis [BR].

The Porter

George Clark Foster of Hawes

George Foster was born on the April 19th 1906 and was the son of a long serving Wensleydale railwayman and the grandson of a Wensleydale railwayman. Having such a family history of working in the railway industry made it a certainty that he too would follow in the footsteps of those two men. He duly did so in June 1920 as a fourteen year old newly left school lad. George worked for fifty years on the railway and on his retirement began writing down his experiences of his life on the line. There follows a transcript of his story titled 'Along the Iron Road' and it is written as he penned it with only minor alterations. e.g. shortening of sentences and the introduction of paragraphs. I must stress that George Foster's grammar and spelling was first class.

Along the Iron Road

T'was in the month of June 1920 at the age of 14 years when life was young and gay and I embarked on a career with the North Eastern Railway, leaving school on the Friday and making the journey on the Saturday morning from Hawes to Gateshead for the purpose of being supplied with a suit of clothing for my position of 'lad' Porter at Hawes. This post was classified as a supernumery.

The day of commencing duty was the following Monday morning. My boyhood visions of the outfitters department at Gateshead were of elaborate enterprise, thinking of carpets, chandeliers, and flower bedecked tables etc. Shop assistants traversing the floors with tape measures hanging loosely around their necks. All this fantasy was for the contrary as enquiries at the station proved to be just the reverse of my expectations. I was instructed by the Station supervisor to enter the door adjacent to where we were standing and at which a confrontation appeared before my very eyes. There were shelves stacked with clothing all of various kinds, the floor was strewn with fire buckets, shunting poles, brake sticks, coal scuttles, dusters, sweeping brushes of all sizes, brooms, scrubbing brushes, floor cloths, pails and many more essentials which were required on the railway. The aroma of that stores dept. mainly consisted of tarbands and paraffin. Eventually I was approached by the storekeeper who took my measurements and fitted me out with the uniform. This comprised of green corduroy trousers, jacket and waistcoat. Yet more to my amazement and fascination was the style of the trousers that had a drop-flap at the front ready for the call of nature on the urinal.

Monday morning arrived and I set out for my first day's work at 8.30 am having three days learning the duties prior to taking over a rostered shift which was 8.30. am to 7.pm with a break for dinner of one hour and a half hour for tea. This constituted an eight hour day. Incidentally, the station was in those days known as 'Hawes Joint' with both North Eastern and Midland trains having running power to and from Northallerton and Skipton.

My duties varied considerably from cleaning and polishing to the loading and unloading of freight traffic and the delivery of local parcels to the town shops twice daily. A considerable amount of Wensleydale cheese was despatched by goods and passenger trains, the cheese coming from the Wensleydale dairy and local farmers. With the mention of farmers, this coincided with the farming industry situated in a very large agricultural area which was comprised mostly of pasture and meadowland; the pastures rising to a height of 1,800 feet above sea level. A vast amount of sheep and cattle could be found grazing all the year round unless weather necessitated the transfer of livestock into lower pastures.

George Foster (centre) at Hawes station with his father extreme right c. 1925

It was a daily occurrence for farmers to despatch milk to various destinations, the main depot for receiving them was Finsbury Park, but quite a number of churns were sent to Manchester, Liverpool, Newcastle and Northallerton. Each night there were six four wheeled barrows of milk churns to despatch at 6.45 pm and these were loaded into the various vans of the passenger train bound for Northallerton which also collected milk en route. It may seem strange to relate that the farm servants were on a rostered basis to assist with the loading of the traffic. This also applied on Sundays as a 'special milk train' was run every Sunday of the year from Northallerton to Hawes and return. The work of loading this traffic was most difficult at times and more especially in the winter months when climatic conditions were most unfavourable having to contend with two or three feet of snow. This was detrimental to the horses and floats coming from the outlying farms to the station with the milk.

Milk being loaded at Aysgarth station for delivery to London the 4th December 1929.
This milk would be bottled and on the doorsteps of London households by the
following morning. Station Master Walls can be seen at the end of the platform.

Time never stood still as the weeks and months rolled by and the approach of payday on a Friday and calling at the Booking Office and drawing the 'princely sum' of twelve to fourteen shillings every week was quite an event. However, after every twelve months service up to the age of 18, an extra 5/- was applied to the basic rate. In the NER, one became more prosperous but that was not in comparison to the work which became increasingly harder especially at the back end of the year when cattle and sheep were the main sources of revenue to the NER and Midland Railways. Something in the order of

5,000 sheep were despatched by special trains pulling 40 wagons to various destinations. On one particular day demand was so large that 4 high sided coke wagons from Skipton were included. I drew the attention of the Stationmaster and raised a strong objection to the conveyance of sheep under such conditions. I told him that "in my opinion the sheep could be roasted alive' prior to the sheep special arriving at Hawes Junction a distance of six miles owing to the fact that the railway was on an incline for the full stretch. The engine(s) having to maintain a full pressure of steam it would be quite unavoidable for red hot cinders to emerge from the engine funnel and fall onto the wool of the sheep. My objections were reported by phone to the control office at Skipton and the wagons were withdrawn for the purpose of loading sheep. Later, farmers requested that milk cows when being loaded and moved, they being covered with tarpaulins to keep the animals warm especially during the night. Sawdust for floor covering could be supplied at 6d per barrow load. One of the most unusual loads was the occasional loading of geese into a cattle wagon to be conveyed from Hawes to Stokesley. The time taken in loading these 'Goosey-Gooseys' was longer than the loading of elephants from the occasional visit by a circus to the town.

One of the most agonising moments during my occupation at Hawes was working to rule which could possibly have resulted in an unhappy ending. In the rules of signalling, if another train was due to follow immediately from one section to another, an extra tail lamp was to be placed on the rear of the proceeding train and then taken off at the terminal point of the train following and this was of course Hawes station. The train was just in motion, but this was due to an oversight on the part of the guard who had given the 'right of way' signal to the driver prior to the completion after the extra tail lamp had to be placed on the guards van. It so happened that I was in the course of the action when in an endeavour to place the lamp in the van, my foot slipped from the footboard due to the frozen snow and ice. I was left hanging to the van door rail with both of my legs dangling between the train and the platform. The crunch was terrific and the staff on duty shouted to me to 'hang on!' This I had to do with determination until the train was brought to a standstill by the guard who had also seen my predicament and applied the Westinghouse hand brake which brought the train to a halt after I had been carried approximately 25 yards. The result of this caused me to swing round with my head coming in to contact with the side rail of the van door. It so happened that I fell onto the level crossing and what I remember after the fall was very little as I had become unconscious within seconds. From that time which was 12.30 pm I knew nothing more until 9 pm when I awoke to find myself at home. There were no ambulances in those days, so I understand I was transferred from the station to my home in the most convenient way and that was by the ordinary parcels delivery barrow. Following recovery after severe bruising of both legs, I was able to resume normal duties within a week of the accident.

On attaining the age of eighteen years of age, the time had arrived for my transfer to an adult post which coincided with the re-opening of Crakehall station following its closure during the 1914-18 Great War. This was quite an isolated station and different in many ways to what I had been accustomed to, I was in another world altogether, yet I had to make the best of it. The recreation I missed most was my beloved game of billiards which was a nightly occurrence during my few years at Hawes and being a member of the first team of the Conservative Club.

There were no sidings to contend with at Crakehall as it was a single line throughout the section from Bedale to Jervaulx. The village was about a mile from the station and of very little interest so far as recreation was concerned. The only enjoyment I found was to visit an inn situated on the Bedale to Newton le Willows main road south of the station and within 100 yards distance from where I was in 'digs' with Mr and Mrs Wood who resided in the house attached to the station. I can recall many happy memories of my stay with them as we used to have an occasional walk to the inn to pass an hour away in the evening if only just for a game of dominoes and a drink of shandy. There were times during daylight when all station duties had been attended to that I was able to assist a farmer in 'turnip snagging' as the field was adjacent to the railway side, but for all the turnips I snagged, I never received any payment from that period to this.

I was in employment quite a few weeks at Crakehall when an opportunity arose through a mutual agreement with a colleague employed at Askrigg station who was prepared to exchange posts with me. This agreement was eventually carried out, but I knew quite well that I was jumping out of the frying pan into the fire as I would be back again where there was plenty of work both on the siding and on the platform. I know this was to my satisfaction in comparison to the monotony of Crakehall. There was very little loading of livestock at Askrigg but the main income traffic consisted of coal, cattle feed, hay and straw. The coal being loaded in what were commonly known as hopper wagons which were placed over the coal cells and released through bottom doors. Following the unloading, the wagons had to be pushed clear of the cells by hand so that the doors could be replaced and secured by the door pins, thus making them ready for return use at the collieries. Fifteen to twenty of these wagons arrived every week and averaged ten tons per wagon. There were many days when one never looked as being employed by N. E. Railway but more like a coal miner working deep down in the bowels of the earth or on the contrary to the resemblance of a member of the Black and White Minstrel Show such was the dust that came out in clouds on the unloading of the wagons. Dust storms arose like smoke from a blast furnace whenever there was a wind blowing irrespective of direction. Soap and hot water was the only solution to the restoration of a local railway employee.

In the course of daily duties, signal lamps had to be placed in all signals and the fuel for such lamps was ordinary paraffin which were lit ready prior to heading for the distant signals three quarters of a mile from the station. The only time I failed this venture was during a gale force wind at the down distant. Having climbed the ladder of about thirty rungs three times attempting to place the lamp, the light became extinguished on each occasion by the velocity of the wind. My temper was becoming more than frayed and on the fourth attempt to my dismay, the light went out once more, I flung the lamp from the top of the ladder and in doing so it came in contact with the track below and was smashed to smithereens. My tale of woe was duly explained to the stationmaster on my return but very little commiseration was forthcoming, so I curtly replied that it would be his turn the next time there was a gale force wind.

Several months after working at Askrigg, I was sent on relief duties to Aysgarth followed by similar duties at Leyburn. A great deal of coal, cattle feed meal and flour etc was being consigned from Leyburn to the Yore Mills Cake and Flour Company situated close to the High Halls. I well remember the name of an employee of the Cake and Flour Company, he was Owen Dinsdale and he must have unloaded thousands of tons of this traffic in his time. Owen was one of those typical Dalesmen of that era. Very sublime and courteous in many ways who loved his pipe and tobacco. Coming into the yard one day Owen saw my mate Geoff Harding and I hanging the stationmaster's stair carpet out on the clothes line. He casually remarked, 'have you started spring cleaning?' This was all due to the filling of the water tank which supplied water to the station toilets, this being a daily occurrence of pumping water into the tank by hand which was normally a ten minute job. I was pumping in the water and my colleague had climbed the ladder into the tank house and after a lapse of 20 to 30 minutes, I shouted in a rather annoyed voice 'How much more?' His reply was 'carry on George, nearly full' Within five minutes of the reply the station master came dashing round to see what we were up to. His uniform hat tipped on the back of his head and his face like a beetroot. I knew immediately something had gone wrong when he exclaimed 'What are you two lads up to?' You've filled more than the water tank, my bathroom is flooded and all the stair carpet is soaked. The origin of this was that Harding had kept his hand over the tank pipe and forced the water into the stationmaster's bathroom. That was the result of our spring cleaning episode, but the day was not completed until we had relaid the stair carpet

Following my stay at Aysgarth was a transfer to Leyburn. This station was well renowned for racehorse traffic and practically everyday of the week racehorses were loaded and unloaded. During the flat racing season, horse specials were run to Manchester, Liverpool, Newcastle, Redcar, Ayr, Chester, Pontefract, York etc. The trainers were mostly resident at Middleham and familiar names were those of Dobson, Peacock and Son, Armstrong, Osbourne and Drake along with those two well known jockeys, W. Nevett and A. Waudby. There were many big winners of established races from those stables which included, The Lincoln, Chester Cup, Ebor Handicap, Northumberland Plate and November Handicap. Some of those winning racehorses are still fresh in my memory such as, Bonny Brighteyes, Polyanthus, Primrose League and Ornamentation and in later years the Derby winner Dante and the National winner Sheila's Cottage. Working with the horses and the trainers was the 'Kick off' to when I became interested in having a flutter and I became a frequent visitor to the Bookies. After six years of working on the Wensleydale line, I must have been considered more mature for in 1926 I was offered a position on the mainline station at Northallerton. Work at Northallerton was very different where north/south express trains thundered through at 60 mph. There was also greater numbers of passengers, great volumes of parcel traffic and freight to be dealt with and many more staff to get to know. My arrival at Northallerton ended my direct involvement with that small branch line of the Yorkshire Dales. Later that year I was involved in the general strike and found times very difficult. It transpired that I could not live in digs on the meagre strike pay being paid so I was compelled to return to Hawes until the end of the strike in the November of 1926.

One of my favourite memories of my time at Northallerton was when I liberated hundreds of racing pigeons on the platform which had earlier arrived from Scotland and the south of England for an international pigeon race. Later I worked at Scarborough and Malton but in 1945 I moved to Thirsk station where I eventually was promoted to Station Inspector. My time at Northallerton, Scarborough and Thirsk is another story.

George Foster releasing a basket of racing pigeons from Northallerton station in 1928

In 1941 George Foster and his wife became part of the wartime evacuee programme when they took in Margaret Chambers and her two sisters who all hailed from Gateshead Co. Durham. There follows a brief résumé of her memories and times living in Wensleydale with the Fosters which all began with a meandering train ride from Northallerton to Askrigg.

Margaret, Mary and Doreen Chambers 1941

The Evacuee

Margaret Arnell [nee Chambers] of Gateshead recalls with a little apprehension but a great deal of happiness those long gone wartime days when hordes of children were seemingly packed off without so much as a thought to all parts of the country to protect them from the expected aerial onslaught. Eleven year old Margaret and her twin sister Mary with their younger sister Doreen were taken by their mother to Gateshead railway station with the obligatory suitcase and label with name attached. Their tearful mother waved them goodbye as they set off to the Yorkshire Dales on an adventure that was to last four long years. By this time Margaret was a 'veteran' of the evacuation programme as this was her second time of being sent away from home. In early 1940 she had been sent to Sowerby near Thirsk but was 'repatriated' by her soldier father who was stationed in the area. A short time later he was killed in France leaving a wife with six children to look after.

Before the three girls left Gateshead, their mother reminded Margaret that if they were to be split up, Margaret must go by herself while her sister Mary was to go with the youngest girl. The reason she was chosen to be the one to live by herself was that she was the oldest. She thought this a trifle unfair as she was only twenty minutes older than her twin, Mary. When it came to the time when they were to be split up, her little sister Doreen was so brave through it all that it made her determined to do her very best for all three of them.

The train set off and arrived in Northallerton where with scores of other children they had to change to another that was travelling down the Wensleydale line. They settled in the tiny smoking steaming train and were soon captivated by each tiny railway station on the way to their unknown destination and by the endless green fields where sheep and cattle grazed lazily. These sights and sounds were new experiences for such children from large towns and cities. They arrived at what turned out to be Askrigg station where after detraining they were formed up into twos and walked crocodile fashion to a school building which she later discovered to be Yorebridge Grammar School. None of them found the next event to be a very pleasant experience for they were all quickly assembled by a rather strict looking nurse and led into a small room where they had a strange smelling liquid rubbed on their hair and washed out. The liquid turned out to be Jeyes Fluid. The Dales folk assumed that all children from large places such as Gateshead, Newcastle and Sunderland must have head lice and so they were treated accordingly. Her mother was very angry when she found out about this unconventional hair treatment. To this day Margaret cannot stand the smell of Jeyes Fluid.

Their next move was by bus to the school at Hardraw and when they arrived she was very surprised at how small it was. It consisted of just two class rooms, one small room for the infants and a larger one for the juniors. The school desks were fixed to the floor where she and her twin along with their little sister were made to sit down. The local inhabitants came to look them over and did so as though they were at an auction mart. They were approached by a lovely friendly looking woman who wanted to take Margaret and her twin sister Mary, but Margaret acted the part of the big sister and insisted that Doreen had to go with Mary to which the woman agreed. This left Margaret alone and she was eventually taken in by a sharp featured woman. Margaret took an instant dislike to the woman who turned out to be quite unfair to her. Quite fortunately her sister Mary's 'home' was quite near to where Margaret was living which made it easier for them to meet and stay in touch. She stayed with the sharp featured woman for nine months after which she was moved to a new 'billet' as it was called in those evacuee days and taken in by a family by the name of Foster who lived in Hawes. Mr. Foster was a retired railway man whose eldest son was also on the railway as a porter and his other son was employed on the railway at Thornaby on Tees. The Foster family treated Margaret as a daughter and gave her all the love and attention that she so missed while being away from her own mother. Their own daughter acted like a big sister to her and she remembers those four years in

Wensleydale living with the Fosters with a great deal of affection. Her twin and younger sister were also looked after with great care and love during their stay in the Dales. In 1945 all girls returned to their mother in Gateshead. To this day Margaret believes that her character was formed by her time spent in the Dales living with the Fosters. She says that part of her heart will always remain in beautiful Wensleydale which began with that meandering train ride from Northallerton to Askrigg railway station.

Ursula Jackson. Passenger Porter

Ursula Jackson was the Passenger porter at Leyburn station from 1941 to 1945 and the station master at the time was Mr. Mattison with Jack Cooper as the goods porter. Ursula recalls her time at Leyburn as being a mix of boredom, fun and extreme hard work. Although she was the passenger porter one of her tasks was to ensure that the sheep arriving from the auction mart were herded into a truck. Oddly enough those flocks arrived on the passenger side of the station therefore it was her task to see to them. Once the sheep had been herded onto the platform, Ursula was expected to count each individual sheep onto the truck and at times it could be rather tricky getting some sort of order with them. The farmers were very keen that numbers tallied and so counting was a sort of hoped for business. If for some reason the numbers didn't tally when all had been herded on to the truck, every single one had to herded off again and recounted back on, one by one. A very tricky and warm job with animals scurrying and dodging everywhere, to say nothing of the dirt and grime. This procedure was carried out in reverse whenever the sheep were going to the auction mart. Ursula stayed on the railway at Leyburn station until the end of the war and awaited the return of her soldier husband from wartime army service. She still has a soft spot for the branch line and treasures the many memories of working at Leyburn and that lively crowd of girls. She now lives in retirement in Spennithorne.

The female staff at Leyburn 1943/44.
Madge Broadley
Audrey Keighly
Ursula Jackson
Margaret Pybus
Barbara Robinson

The Signalman

Alan Hiscock.

Fifteen year old Alan Hiscock started work in 1955 as a Lad Porter at Northallerton station. One of the first jobs that he was given was to record entries in the log book which were always to be found in the signal cabins and also to act as a general 'gofer'. He began his signalling career at Ainderby station and it was there that he was introduced to the Tyler Electric Token Signalling system. It was to be Alan who finally closed that signal box down on October 19th 1986 when the line was being downgraded. The signal box survives to this day and now forms part of the Alston railway in Northumberland.

A short time after starting at Ainderby Alan transferred to Aysgarth where he came under the wing of Stationmaster Mr. Milner. In the winter months, Alan stayed at digs with Mrs. King in nearby Carperby as travel to and from Northallerton to the Dales was at best unreliable and of course early starts precluded him taking any form of public transport.

Aysgarth station had quite a large car parking area and with tourism in the Dales flourishing due to the increase in car ownership, the Rail authorities made the most of its use. From Mondays to Fridays both Station Master Milner and Alan would act as car park attendants charging 1/- per car and 2/6d for a coach, on Saturdays and Sundays they would do the same but were on a commission for all vehicles parked. All monies collected were dutifully handed over to British Railways for accounting, after which Alan and Mr. Milner were paid a percentage. After a particularly good weekend, Alan could receive something approaching an extra £4 in his wage packet, which equalled two thirds of his weekly wage. The irony of all this was that both of them were unwittingly aiding the demise of train travel to the Dales by assisting with car parking facilities.

In the closed season, the Station Master would often take Fridays off [quite unofficially] and that was when Alan took the opportunity to man the signal box to gain experience while at the same time carrying out limited duties of the station master. In 1959 he was promoted to signalman at Aysgarth which was to be a start to a long career in signalling and signal management. By the time of his promotion there was only one scheduled train passing each day, and once it had departed down line, the signal box would be left unmanned. However if a train was on the line for whatever reason, extra pay was awarded as 'four hour block time' viz. time spent in the signal cabin up to the four hours duration. A ruse often worked by Alan was to get some of the track walkers to take a track walker's trolley and leave it on the line, thus creating 'traffic' which had to be controlled. With such ruses he got his extra pay. Sometimes the chase for earning extra pay worked against Alan and other signalmen. A request was often made to the shuntermen to move a set of wagons to another section or where ever, only to be met by the reply 'We'll do it tomorrow for you' The reason for doing it tomorrow? They were finishing early so that they could get in a spell of farm work to earn some extra money themselves. Quite frustrating for Alan but it showed the low level of wages paid to the ordinary railwayman and the gaps in managerial control. Not only did many line workers take on extra work, there were a variety of spare time ruses whilst on duty. Rabbit snaring, gardening, hair cutting and even orders for crocheting and knitting were taken. Signalman Nessfield Hartley was renowned for his knitting skills and during the clothes rationing days of the Second World War, he would cut off a 'holy' foot from a worn sock and knit a new seamless one in its place. It may not have been the same colour but it suited the purpose admirably. He even once knitted a tie, but it was a one off job and it was for himself. Such was his prowess that he often won competitions when other knitters were women.

N.B. Many folk have wondered how Ness was given such an unusual name as Nessfield. Apparently it all began some 200 years ago when the matriarch of the Hartley family gave birth to a boy after a romantic liaison with the son of Squire Nessfield of Grosmont. But the father refused to marry her as he deemed her to be beneath his class. The girl retaliated by Christening her son Nessfield after the family name of the father, to let it be known who was responsible. That rare Christian name lay dormant until the mid 1890s when Nessfield late of the Wensleydale railway was born.

Wool or fleece collecting was one of the myriad of tasks taken on by the motor drivers of the line and in early summer, drivers were busy collecting the fleeces of the thousands of sheep that had been sheared from the scores of farms in the Dales. A collection of wool was known as a 'sheet' and after being collected and weighed, it was loaded onto a railway wagon. Alan recalls a time when motor driver Mick Heseltine arrived at the station with four sheets of wool which were then loaded into the goods train for delivery. The driver of the engine reversed into the engine shed with the barrier wagon to his rear instead of in the front and then he applied a blast of steam power. The sudden burst of high pressure steam from the pressure pipe [funnel] blew forty or more tiles off the roof causing considerable external damage.

Alan moved eventually from the Wensleydale line to Middlesbrough and in 1995 retired ending his career as senior Signalling Manager for Railtrack North east.

Alan on the steps of Ainderby signal box.

A goods train arriving at Wensley

A signalman at Ainderby handing over the single line tablet to the driver c 1950

Alan Hiscock as a callow eighteen year old youth at Northallerton.

Eric Irving. Signalman

 Eric Irving started his railway career in 1941 as a fourteen year old youth and as was the usual case, he began from the lowly but indispensable position of Lad Porter working at Hawes with a starting wage of 19/6 rising to £3/12/6 at sixteen. His father Jack Irving was the goods agent at the station who later became the office clerk. Hawes was a joint LMS and LNER station and the buildings and signal box were of LMS design The station staff were LNER and the permanent way staff LMS.

Eric soon made it to porter and worked alongside such characters as 'Pasty' Mason who was a qualified signalman of many years standing. He earned the nick-name Pasty as apparently he was very fond of meat pasties which almost seemed to be his staple diet. Pasty always wore a collared shirt and a dickey bow when at work and his signal cabin was spick and span, with everything that could be polished, gleaming brightly and was very much his pride and joy. Anyone entering his cabin with soiled boots was told not to wander all around the cabin and to try and keep the floor clean. His philosophy was that as he might have to spend anything up to ten or twelve hours in that cabin, it should be as comfortable and clean as possible.

Pasty taught Eric that signal levers were never pulled with bare hands but covered by a cloth as the sweat from the palms could cause the levers to go rusty. He was also very much a man of the old school and took it upon himself to rein in the coarser side of the young men with whom he worked at Hawes station. Eric recalls one young chap coming out with a stream of ripe expletives in the presence of Pasty and was soon given a lecture on the bad habits of swearing with the quietly spoken rebuke 'A young man like you shouldn't go around using language like that my lad'. It was usually enough to chasten the young man enough for him to remember not to swear in Pasty's company ever again. However the warning probably didn't have the slightest effect on his language when he was with others.

By the time Eric had got into his stride at Hawes, the war had been raging for more than two years and although he was too young to serve in the regular armed forces, like almost every other exempt rail worker of a certain age he was expected to volunteer for the Home Guard. He duly joined the 2nd Battalion Green Howards [HG] and although they were all as keen as mustard, his time in the Home Guard followed that of a 'Dad's Army' episode. Porter/signalman Jackie Moore or 'Shooky' as he was known was the platoon quarter master sergeant and as such he was responsible for equipment. Although the standard rifle for the troops was the Lee Enfield .303 Shooky had as his very own and very personal weapon, a .22 rifle. This he kept in the signal cabin and he would use it to take pot-shots at rabbits to augment his weekly meat ration. He once loaned the rifle to Eric and told him to go and bag a couple of rabbits. Eric strode off and got a rabbit clear in his sights, but didn't have the heart to shoot it, so he went meatless. One story that Shooky often regaled Eric and the rest with was the time he went on a drinking spree with a motor driver and arrived back at the station very much the worse for wear. Fortunately the circus was in town and the motor driver managed to bed Shooky down amongst the straw in the trailer the elephants had occupied during their journey to Hawes. He must have been well and truly away as he later made no mention of the smell.

Wartime regulations were in full swing especially with the transporting of livestock for the sales from August to December. One of Eric's jobs was to get a goodly number of sheep onto the wagon and his trick was to grab one and pull it into the wagon which made the rest follow. There were also the occasional bull sales and it fell to Eric to somehow get the beast into the sales ring. He would somehow lead the beast to the open gate and when the bull got somewhere near it, he simply ran! One of the ruses they got up to from time to time; was when they were seeing off newly weds on the train to the sound of detonators [time expired]. Just before the happy couple climbed aboard and the whistle was blown, several detonators would be laid on the line and the bride and groom would begin their married life to the sound of a series of explosions. This usually went down very well, but unfortunately on one 'wedding day', the scheme, like the detonators backfired. On one wedding day and unbeknown to the staff, a farm worker with a horse and cart was quietly muck spreading in a field near the line. As the detonators exploded the startled horse bolted and galloped full tilt to the nearest gate which fortunately was wide open and it ran straight through it. The cart was wrecked in the ensuing mêlée, resulting in the irate farmer claiming compensation.

Eric Irving late qualified as a porter /signalman and went to Kirkby Stephen for a spell and then back to Hawes for a short time he was then moved to the signal box at Boroughbridge Road and then to Low Gates Northallerton. He retired in 1990 after working for more than forty nine years with the railway. Eric now lives in retirement in Northallerton.

Hawes Station staff 1946
Beckwith Thompson, Porter, Bob Hind,Porter, Eric Irving, Porter, John Irving,Clerk
Tom Thackray, Station Master, John Mason, Signalman, Jacky Moor, Porter/Signalman

The Signalling System.

I am grateful to Alan Hiscock for this written description of the signalling system used on the Wensleydale line.

The system used to control trains was known as the Electric Token Block but was only applicable to certain sections of the line. These sections were; Ainderby-Leeming Bar, Bedale-Leyburn, Leyburn-Wensley, Wensley- Aysgarth, Aysgarth-Askrigg, Askrigg-Hawes. [The section between Leeming Bar and Bedale was double line] The section from Northallerton to Ainderby used the Transient Block System, sometimes known as the Sweeping the Track System and was one of only two sections of rail line to use this system in the UK, the other being in Lincolnshire.

The Electric Token Block System.

If the signalman at Leeming Bar had received the 'train out' of the section signal for the preceding train and the Block Indicator was in the normal position i.e. 'tablet in' he would then call the attention of the signalman at Ainderby. On confirmation he would give him the proper 'Is Line Clear signal' which indicated the type of train. If the line was clear and no other train expected from Northallerton the signalman at Ainderby would acknowledge the signal and hold the Block plunger in the box in the down position. This would allow the signalman at Leeming Bar to withdraw a tablet from the Block Instrument. After obtaining a token the signalman at Leeming Bar would then clear his signals for the train to carry on to Ainderby and hand the token contained in a pouch held by a large metal loop to the driver giving him the authority to proceed. He must then send the 'train entering section' signal and await an acknowledgement. When the train had passed through Ainderby complete with tail lamp, the Ainderby signalman would notify Leeming Bar then replace the token into the Block Instrument and send the train 'out of the section' signal, while holding the plunger at which the signalman at Leeming Bar would return the commentator to the normal position.

Herbert Jobling operating the Electric Block Indicator from Leeming Bar signal box.

Alan Hiscock explains that this somewhat convoluted procedure took place all along the line on each occasion a train was running, but in practice it was much simpler in its execution and was very efficient.

THE SIGNALBOX BELL CODE IS PLANNED SO THAT EACH
SIGNAL CONFORMS TO A PARTICULAR TRAIN HEADCODE

BRITISH STANDARD HEADLAMP CODE

The Southern Region uses special codes made up from sheet iron discs, the purpose of which is not to display the *kind* of train but to indicate to signalmen and others where it is bound for. The Eastern Section of the Eastern Region also uses these white metal discs in daylight hours, in conformity with the standard code (*left*) on main lines, and, with purple discs also, as route indicators in the London suburban area. The London Midland Region uses white metal discs in conformity with the standard code on locomotives fitted with electric light during hours of daylight. All other British Railways Regions use the standard headlamp code shown here.

Electric trains in suburban areas use special codes as route indicators.

STANDARD SIGNALBOX BELL CODE

Class of Train	Message	Beats on Bell
	Call attention	1
	is line clear for:—	
A	Express passenger train	4
B	Ordinary passenger train	3—1
	Branch passenger train	1—3
C	Non-passenger train composed entirely of vehicles conforming to coaching stock requirements	1—3—1
	Express freight train pipe-fitted throughout with automatic brake operative on not less than half the vehicles	3—1—1
	Empty coaching stock train	2—2—1
D	Express freight train with automatic brake operative on not less than one third of the vehicles...	5
E	Express freight train with automatic brake operative on not less than four vehicles, or Express freight train with a limited load of vehicles **not** fitted with continuous brake	1—2—2
F	Express freight train **not** fitted with continuous brake	3—2
G	Light engine...	2—3
	Light engines coupled together	1—1—3
H	Through freight or ballast train	1—4
J	Mineral or empty wagon train	4—1
K	Freight train stopping at intermediate stations	3
	Branch freight train	1—2
	Freight train requiring to stop in section	2—2—3
	*Train entering section	2
	†Train out of section, or obstruction removed	2—1
	Obstruction danger	6
	Train passed without tail lamp	9(‡) 4—5(§)
	Train divided	5—5
	Stop and examine train	7
	Closing Signal Box	7—5—5
	Opening Signal Box	5—5—5

*Rear box warns box ahead that train has passed.
†Box ahead notifies rear box that train has arrived.
(‡) To box ahead. (§) To box in rear.

Class of Train	Description
A	Express passenger, newspaper or break-down train; express diesel car; snow plough on duty; fire brigade on duty; light engine proceeding to assist disabled train.
B	Ordinary passenger, branch passenger or "mixed" train; rail motor (loaded or empty); ordinary passenger or parcels diesel car; breakdown train not on duty.
C	Parcels, fish, fruit, livestock, milk or other perishable train composed entirely of vehicles conforming to coaching stock requirements; express freight, livestock, perishable or ballast train pipe fitted throughout with automatic vacuum brake operative on not less than half of the vehicles; empty coaching stock (not specially authorised to carry "A" code).
D	Express freight, livestock, perishable or ballast train with not less than one third vacuum braked vehicles piped to the engine.
E	Express freight, livestock, perishable or ballast train with not less than four vacuum braked vehicles piped to the engine; or express freight of *limited load* not fitted with continuous brake.
F	Express freight, livestock or ballast train not fitted with continuous brake.
G	Light engine(s) or engine with not more than two brake vans.
H	Through freight or ballast trains not running under "C", "D", "E" or "F" conditions.
J	Mineral or empty wagon train.
K	Pick-up or branch freight, mineral or ballast train.

The lamp and bell signals for all signalmen denoting the type of train.

Bill Redhead. Aiskew Gatekeeper.

Bill Redhead was born on Tyneside and in the early part of his working life was employed as a trackman/platelayer in the rail yard of Bolden Colliery in County Durham. Poor health compelled him to leave heavy manual work and do what was described as 'Welfare work'. As a result of his leaving Bolden he and his family came to live near Aiskew village where Bill was given the job of running the Aiskew Gates. Although strictly speaking it was a set of gates he controlled, there were a number of signal levers to be operated Therefore, Bill Redhead although not a signalman but allowing for the authors right to a modicum of licence, he is accorded his place among that fraternity.

The face of experience. Bill Redhead at the doorway of the Aiskew cabin

Brian Redhead the distinguished writer and journalist currently writing for the Darlington and Stockton Times newspaper, is the son of that crossing keeper/signalman, the late Bill Redhead. Brian's father manned the crossing at Aiskew for twenty one years and the young Brian spent many a happy summer's school holiday and not a few winter evenings with his father in that sparse and austere cabin. This led him to become steeped in the lore and the romance of the Wensleydale line. Brian recorded his memories of those days with his father in the Town and Country notes by 'Spectator' of the D&S Times on Friday November 26th 1982. There follows a transcript of that report by Brian and it is written in his well known very readable and inimitable style and one can almost feel the anguish he felt when the curtain finally fell on the line.

41

I have my own very special memories of Mr. Plummer's Branch line, they are precious recollections, now so distant as to be almost a dream of a boy of eleven or twelve spending long summer holidays and [homework permitting] the occasional story of a winter evening in and around a little signal box at Aiskew crossing. Its exact building date is obscure, but it seems to have stood guard forever at the side of this busy main road between Bedale and Northallerton. Compared with its big brothers a mile away on either side, it is just big enough to swing the proverbial cat. It has only eight levers, some permanently out of commission. Officially, I suppose, it is not even classed as a proper signal box, being more a gatehouse. To me though, it is a repository of past glories-the starting point of my present obsessive interest in railways, both full size and miniature.

There have been many books and articles on the Wensleydale branch [including one for which I was asked to supply pictures] but none has captured the sheer flavour and atmosphere of daily life on the line as my father and others once knew it. My father spent twenty one years in that box, seeing hundreds of trains safely on their way and making friends with a generation of bus drivers and motorists forced to stop at the gates. The line was already on its last legs, having lost its passenger service a few years earlier when I got to know it in the late 1950s. But it still had more appeal and character in every few yards of track than its emaciated skeleton possess today.

Red Discs.

All signal boxes were romantic places for me at that age, but the Aiskew box was something special because it was so small. It was a cosy enclosed world bounded by calendars, timetables, train instruments with brass trimmings and official looking notices by one C.M. Jenkin Jones. In high summer you felt like a ripening tomato in a hothouse. In the winter, rain battered the window panes, driving snow piled up against the door and frosts froze gates and points solid. You could then defeat even the draughts howling up through the lever frame by roasting yourself in front of the big black stove while a paraffin lamp guttered on the wall above your head. Beside the window hung little red discs like milk bottle tops. They were detonators-dangerous warning devices which exploded violently under the train wheels. Hiding behind one of the train instruments was a pile of booklets, many with buff coloured covers and all with a British Railway motif. They seemed to consist mainly of confusing amendments to amendments with little erratum slips stuck here and there just to make it more difficult. The most interesting was a little black volume-a 1950 rule book embodying such sensible restrictions as 'hot water not to be emitted from engines in tunnels' and advising on 'arms, use of' in hand signalling. On the shelf stood the LNER paraffin-powered hand lamp whose top could be turned to produce four coloured lenses. Beside the telephone hung a fading postcard bearing the dots and dashes like Morse code, by which other boxes were rung up. There was a lovely wooden armchair with a curved back, the sort you see in cowboy films, as well as a battered old bench and cupboard holding everything from oily rags to washing powder.

Spark fires.

Then there were the smells. Unforgettable combinations of food, chemicals and pure 'railwayana' as well as more mysterious smells from which seemed to emanate from the very wood of the building. Paraffin, metal polish, black lead and boot polish. Burnt toast with a fork fashioned from twisted signal wire. Tomatoes and eggs sizzling. Above all the characteristic pong of creosote from worn out old sleepers used for firewood. Everything was exciting in those days. Boyhood diaries testify to the calamities of over energetic steam engines. More than one line side fire caused by stray sparks had to be beaten out with shovels. Some firemen were generous with gifts of coal, kicking huge chunks off the footplate as the engine passed. Platelayer's petrol driven vehicles commonly called bogies, but known to unromantic officialdom as mechanised rail trolleys, scurried here and there like beetles. Fishplates clanged, hammers thudded against wooden keys, sleepers creaked under the weight of hobnailed boots.

Guard's vans in those days when freight trains had them, were cosy refuges as their tail lamps disappeared into the thick fog. Troop trains sometimes ran at dead of night at week ends. They always seemed much longer than ordinary trains-endless brightly lit, maroon painted cavalcades containing hundreds of khaki uniformed men well equipped with beer bottles as well as rifles and Bren guns.

Black Stove.

Occasionally an engine would disgrace itself by jumping the rails at the top of Wensleydale and for my father that could mean a shift of almost 24 hours. Lights and fires in the cabins all along the line would stay on until the gigantic breakdown crane rumbled by. Cap badges then were orange coloured. Drivers wore overalls and greasetop caps. Other railway uniforms were generally slack, snug and warm with bright silver buttons. One or two station masters might even have kept top hats for VIP occasions. My father was proud of his uniform and proud of his cabin. True to his army tradition of spit and polish he kept the handles of the levers gleaming and black frame itself in similar condition. The old box is visible as I write in the gathering dusk, but it is at the mercy of change. There seems to be a conspiracy afoot to change its character to rip out its insides. They started by fitting hideous wire mesh around the windows, they then tore out the big black stove and took away a diagram of lines dating from 1908. The place is no longer safe even from vandals, having been burgled at least three times to my knowledge.
Ah but what memories! Few kids can have been so lucky. Looking at the exhibits in railway museums can never compare with having grown up with the real things.

Brian Redhead was to lament in the very same newspaper of the official 'vandalism' wrought by the demolition company who ripped down the old gatehouse signal box that was so dear to his heart. An article 'Shabby death of a small piece of railway history' was written by Brian and to reprise just three of the paragraphs in the newspaper shows the dismay and the heartbreak felt by Brian.

Darlington & Stockton Times. 8th June 1985.

If anyone in the last few weeks had sneaked into the disused gatehouse at Aiskew after dark looking for relics, they would not have got a cold sausage. They simply would have disappeared into a yawning hole in the floor where the levers used to be.

That was the ultimate indignity of this railway equivalent of a sentry box. To be stripped, gutted deserted and left to die mourned by no one except those enthusiasts inside and outside British Rail who appreciated how well built its signal boxes of wood and brick were. After which, the site where generations of railwaymen worked hand operated gates, lit paraffin lamps and pulled off signals fell silent once more, interrupted only by the peremptory warbling of the automatic system which had been inevitable in its coming for years.

Brian did ask the rail authorities why the empty box could not have stayed in position after the automatic level crossing had been installed. A member of the British Rail Headquarters staff told him rather sniffily "that rates would still have to be paid on the building if it were not removed". So that sentry box of yore was unceremoniously taken down.

A 'smokin' steam engine thunders past Bill Redhead's Gate house.

Bill's ' 'Sentry box' in its heyday.

June 1985.
Official 'vandalism' begins.
The demolition of the
cabin at Aiskew.
A sad sight for many
but especially for
Brian Redhead.

Passengers alight at Redmire
from an excursion organised by
British Rail from York to the Dales
on September 16th 1978.
This was one of
three excursions run in 1978.
The other two were Dalesrail trips
by theYorkshire Dales
National Parks Committee.

The same train passing through Aiskew gates.

A reasonably full eight car Dalesrail train but obviously several carriages too long, standing at Bedale station on the 17th June 1978 awaiting clearance to travel on to Leyburn and then Redmire, the return leg of an excursion from York. This train consisted of refurbished DMU stock.

The Trackman

The Trackman is a generic word for a man who worked on and walked the permanent way of the railways. On the permanent way, those men were known as, track walkers, lengthmen and gangers but officially as platelayers. Whatever they were called, they were the men who kept the rails, sleepers, points, fencing and anything to do with track in a good working condition and very often carried out in blazing sunshine or howling gales and snow.

Harry Hartley 'Track walker'.

Harry Hartley was the son of signalman Nessfield Hartley and also the grandson of a North Yorkshire railwayman and quite naturally he followed them into the 'trade'. His father worked at Leyburn as a signalman from 1930 until his retirement some thirty years later. Harry received his schooling at the local council school in Leyburn, but by the age of thirteen his education was deemed 'complete' and he left to find work. Although not born there, Harry always thinks of Leyburn as his home.

Like so many men in the 1930s, the Second World War interrupted Harry's life and he was eventually called up and joined the Royal Engineers. He was sent to the Middle East where he was captured during the fierce fighting in the Western desert and spent three years as a prisoner in Italy and Germany. At the end of the war he was repatriated and arrived back in England ready to start afresh. He immediately began the task of finding a job and actually applied for a job on the railway whilst still wearing his army uniform. Harry is convinced that being in the Royal Engineers helped him to get a job in the engineering department at Darlington station. He began work as a platelayer on the Permanent Way at Oaktree which is a section of the line between Eaglescliffe and Darlington. He soon found that working the permanent way meant a lot of walking and walk he did in the ensuing years.

In 1950, after two years of working on the Darlington district he went to work at Aysgarth on the Wensleydale line. His job was to walk the eleven and half miles of track between Redmire and Hawes and everyday that he was on duty, come hail or shine he was there walking. Although the permanent way was the main function of his job, the walker was expected to inspect the fencing and check for subsidence of the track and the state of the sleepers. One old hand at the job warned Harry to check for dead sheep that had apparently been run over by a train which would almost invariably result in the farmer making a claim for compensation. Very often the sheep had deliberately been left there by a less than honest farmer. On many occasions Harry found a sheep that had been killed by a train, but he would quickly get his spade and bury it before the farmer found out that his animal had been on the track. So there was a shade of venality from both sides. On one occasion a racehorse special from Scotland to Leyburn ran into a flock of eighty three sheep that were ambling along the line. Fortunately only a few of the sheep were killed, but when the footplate crew got out to check the damage, they discovered that a section of the fence had been broken away by the farmer so as to let the sheep graze the fresh grass. On being informed of the broken fence the farmer would usually decline to put in a claim for compensation for his dead animals.

When the passenger service ceased in 1954, Harry still walked the line up to Hawes but for only two days a week, the rest of the week he walked in the opposite direction toward Spennithorne. He continued on this section until 1958 when he applied for a job at Danby Wiske on the Northallerton to Darlington section of the line. Eventually Harry Hartley became the Northallerton Branch Secretary of the NUR until his retirement. Harry also served as the Chairman of the Bench of Northallerton Magistrates.

John Braithwaite Platelayer/Signalman.

 John Braithwaite was born at Askrigg on the 20th August 1911. Always known as Jack, he joined the railway as a junior platelayer at Askrigg on the Wensleydale line in 1930. He was soon learning the rigours and heavy duties of the job, but also assimilated to the camaraderie that was peculiar to plate layers. In 1940 he decided on a change of jobs and trained to become a porter/signalman and moved to Aysgarth and Redmire. Jack remembers the severe winter of 1947 and the problems it caused to all aspects of the railway. On one occasion he and several other railwaymen went in search of a train that had been abandoned by the crew and passengers and when it was found, it was covered so deeply in the snow that it was left until the weather improved and depth of snow had abated.

In 1948 Jack Braithwaite was promoted to signalman instructor at Catterick Bridge on the Richmond Line. Jack had two brothers who worked on the Wensleydale line, Herbert who became a porter signalman at Wensley, and Matthew who became a porter signalman at Aysgarth.
Jack married the daughter of James Metcalfe who was also a platelayer of the Wensley stretch of line and was reputed to have track-walked 85,000 miles in his time as a platelayer. In the First World War, Jim Metcalfe served with the army in France and worked on the military railways where his experience was of great value to the military rail authorities.

Middle section gang 1940s. L toR
Joe Percival Redmire, Jack Braithwaite Redmire, Jim Metcalfe Redmire,
George Parsley Leyburn, Harry Hutchinson Wensley.

Fred Severs freight guard [right]
with a group of plate layers at Askrigg. 1920s His son Arthur worked as a lad
porter and also as a casual worker on the line.

Middle Section gang 1930s L to R
George Parsley, Harry Hutchinson, Jim Metcalfe, Eddie Dawson Leyburn,
Joe Percival, Other 2 unknown

George Parsley at Leyburn station shortly after his retirement

Like Railway

Father

Like Railway

Son

The Wensleydale
Railway Weighells.

Without doubt the most famous name associated with the Wensleydale line was that of Weighell. Altogether four male members from three generations of the Weighell family worked on the branch line, William, Thomas, Sidney and Maurice.

William Weighell. Guard

William Weighell the patriarch of the family was born at Osmotherley near Northallerton and started his working days on the Wensleydale branch line as a shunter/guard and eventually progressed to passenger guard. He married Fanny Barker and they had three sons and four daughters. William was extremely active in the railway union long before the union was officially recognised, which was a daunting task given the animosity by the owners to such a body. He persevered and eventually was elected as the branch treasurer. William was fondly remembered on the branch line for his hard work, courtesy and not least for his immaculate uniform.
William Weighell died in 1957.

Thomas Weighell. Signalman

Thomas Weighell the eldest of William and Fanny's sons was born in 1893 and joined the NER in 1911 as a signal box boy. Thomas had hardly got used to the idea of working for a living when he was involved in a rail strike brought about by the struggle for union recognition. Due to his activities during the strike, 'he was moved out of the way' to Selby. During the First World War he and his brother Hammond served in the army and when they both arrived home safely, Thomas had been so affected by his experiences in the war that he moved from preaching in the pulpit where he had been acting as a lay preacher to preaching socialism on the soap box which to him was akin to Christianity. Although keeping his Christian beliefs, he had turned his oratory to defending the workers. A fiery but principled union man was in the making. When Thomas finally married, the twin beliefs of Christianity and Socialism proved to be stumbling blocks both for him and his bride. Whenever they tried to set up home, landlords were reluctant to have a crusading preacher-socialist as a tenant so the couple were compelled to live with his uncle, Robert Barker, who was the foreman at Kendrew's farm near Northallerton. They eventually found a furnished terraced house in Gladstone Street Northallerton and settled down to a more orderly married life. Thomas rose to become a signalman of some authority and renown. He then followed in his father's footsteps taking on the mantle of union representative and in 1935 eventually was elected onto the NUR executive committee. He then became secretary and chief negotiator of the LNER Council which was almost a full time job. By 1938 his work as a signalman meant that he was given a lot of relief work and he was even given a vehicle travelling allowance [a bicycle] so that he could get to the many signal boxes in the Northallerton district. Apart from his union work he was elected to the prestigious post of Chairman of Magistrates Court Northallerton. He was awarded the BEM in 1955 and the MBE in 1966.

Thomas Weighell died in 1977.

Sidney Weighell. NUR. General Secretary.

Sidney Weighell *(known as Bogie Weighell)* the eldest son of Thomas was born in Northallerton on the 31st March 1922 and was without doubt the most famous railwayman of the North East of England. He was steeped in Railway Union business long before he was old enough to work for a living, as he was pressed into helping his father with union business. Sidney, who excelled at football and cricket, joined the railway in 1939 as an apprentice in the road motor department at Thirsk for a wage of 8/- per week. He then changed to working first as an engine cleaner and then as a fireman at Northallerton. He has pleasant memories of frying kippers or bacon and eggs on the [clean] shovel held in the firebox on his many journeys up and down the Dale. Strangely for such a union dominated family, it was 1941 before he even bothered to attend a branch union meeting [held at the Durham Ox pub in Northallerton] and then it was to protest at the rotten shift system being worked. It was that innocuous meeting that set Sidney on the way to the highest position in the NUR. That same year he was elected onto the branch committee and was soon asked to be the secretary. His future career was being mapped out.

Sidney took the decision to qualify as a driver so that he would be able to experience from a practical and first hand view, the problems faced by that grade of railwayman. He recalls one shift when a young slip of a lad was acting as his fireman. They set off from Northallerton to travel to Garsdale and as routine, Sidney asked the lad if he had topped up the water tank. To their mutual dismay, the lad admitted that he had forgotten. There was no way the train would be able to make it up the gradients without plenty of water so some quick but unorthodox thinking was reached. By guile and by wit, Sid arranged with the driver of an engine which had plenty of water that was travelling back to Northallerton, [most of the journey had been downhill], to exchange engines with his at a suitable passing point. [The request was highly illegal] After a bit of complicated shunting, the task was completed and trains departed both with different engines. Queries and questions were later asked by engine inspectors, but no one did find out what exactly happened on that day. That episode was a salutary lesson for that young fireman of the importance of the fireman's duties.

Sidney was a keen all round sportsman and his skills as a footballer were such that he was spotted by a Sunderland FC talent scout and eventually played for several seasons for the Weirsiders reserve team. In terms of hours worked for earnings, Sidney earned more for playing football one day a week as a Sunderland reserve than he did working for the railway full time. As age and lack of time caught up with him, he ended his footballing days playing for Brompton, a local team near Northallerton that duly went on to win every cup going in the local league.

Sidney Weighell in full
flow addressing a rally
at Central Hall
Westminster during
a'No Cuts' campaign
1981.

Sidney married Margaret Hunter in 1949 and they had two children, Jennifer and Anthony. In June 1954 he was elected as a full time official of the NUR and resigned from the railway. He moved his family to St. Albans, due to his southern based union work and spent many hours driving on the open roads. In 1956 tragedy struck. Sidney and his wife were involved in a horrific traffic accident which caused the death of Margaret and their daughter Jennifer. After that trauma, Sidney threw all his efforts into the union work and strove to lead the union from the very top. Famously he once said, 'When you have experienced such tragedy, you can face up to anything else that life throws at you'. Sidney remarried in 1959. In 1965 he was elected Assistant General Secretary to Sidney Green of the NUR a post he held for ten years. In 1975 he was elected General Secretary of the NUR, a post he held for eight years. In his time as the General Secretary he had many memorable and Titanic debates [he was a fine orator] with other union leaders such as Arthur Scargill at the annual TUC Congress, and often came out on top in those encounters and fought uncompromisingly to keep the Union clear of the hard left within its ranks. It is fair to say that those confrontations and his early departure from the Union Executive, probably cost Sidney Weighell the knighthood that is often bestowed on union leaders after leaving office.

Sid Weighell .

On his retirement he took to writing his book 'A Hundred Years of Railway Weighells', an interesting and deep insight into his time as a railwayman, his family and as a union official in the NUR. The title of the book reflects the number of years served by William, Thomas, Sidney and Maurice Weighell which ran to a grand total of 176 years service.
Sidney Weighell died in January 2002.

A contemporary
newspaper cartoon of
Sid Weighell

Maurice Weighell Engine driver

Maurice Weighell *(known as Gear Weighell)* was born in 1924 and was the second child of the Weighell family. Maurice began his railway life in 1940 at the age of sixteen in the locomotive department at Northallerton. His first job was working with Bill Gordon the boilersmith helping to patch the sides of tank engines. Within a year he had qualified as a passed fireman and eventually began 'work with the shovel' on the Wensleydale line. Seventeen was a little younger than the norm to begin 'firing' but the manpower shortages due to the war compelled the authorities to lower the age limits. After working on the shunting engines of the line he worked on the passenger trains and freight services. He then followed his brother Sidney to Darlington. One highlight for Maurice was when he acted as fireman on a Gresley Pacific loco on the Wensleydale line. He says that it caused a few people to turn their heads in wonderment. Like most firemen, Maurice learned to drive by watching and being instructed by the driver. When the driver was satisfied that his fireman showed some commonsense and ability, he would let the 'lad' have a drive. Conversely, experienced drivers liked to think they could still do a decent job 'firing' and so they would spend a short while shovelling [but only a short while].

Maurice passed the driver's exam in 1951 and at first acted as cover for sick drivers. He then had a short spell in 'control' at Darlington but that didn't suit him and less than a year later he was back on the footplate. Like his brother Sidney, he became the Northallerton branch secretary of the NUR.

In 1961 Maurice was promoted to full time driver at Thornaby, but was at the bottom of the 'heap' and had to work his way up, that is, he had to do many of the old menial and dirty tasks shunned by the older drivers. He recalls how when he began work at Thornaby, the engine sheds were the very latest in modern equipment and cleanliness, but when told to report to the older sheds nearby, it was like going back a hundred years in time. Everything from the conditions, equipment and lack of facilities were exactly as they might have been in the 1860s. His arrival coincided with the introduction of the diesel engined trains and Maurice took to driving the new engines with ease and like others before him never missed the old steamers one little bit.

Maurice Weighell retired in 1989 and now lives in Middlesbrough.

A Trio of
Gaythorpes

Richard Gaythorpe. Porter

Another well known name connected with the line was the Gaythorpe family of which three generations found employment along its tracks. The first was Richard Gaythorpe who began his working life as a porter on the Northallerton-Leeming Lane link in 1883, thirty five years after it had been opened in 1848 the station acquiring the name of Leeming Bar in 1902. Richard worked on the branch line until his retirement in

1947.

Richard Gaythorpe [centre back row] with the Leeming Lane staff. C. 1885

Harold Gaythorpe Signalman

Richard's son Harold was destined to follow his father onto the railway and on the Wensleydale line. He began work just before the outbreak of the Great War. After serving in the army Harold returned to 'duty' in the signal box at Leeming Bar and was the signalman during the station's heyday of both passenger and goods on what was one of the busiest level crossings on the entire line. Not least because it had the 'Great North Road' interceding in the operations of rail traffic. Until the opening of the A1 by-pass in the 1960s the Great North Road bisected the level crossing and the opening and closing of the gates became a balancing act of careful timing. In those earlier times the gates were opened and closed by a large hand operated wheel, rather like a ship's steering wheel which took some wielding. In the days of passenger services, trains ran sometimes as late as 10pm and judging the traffic for closing the gates especially in the dark winter nights was a matter of even finer judgment than during the day. The 'other' shift signalman was William Archer who regarded Harold's signal control first class as did other work colleagues who knew Harold. Over the years they all said that he was the most reliable and conscientious of workers. Latterly, Herbert Jobling who was a motor driver at Bedale became one of the 'Bar's' signalmen.

Without doubt, Harold was a stalwart of the railway, but almost as important was his gardening. Not just the garden that he tended at his railway cottage, but a plot of land by the side of the track acquired from the railway company. There he grew all manner of vegetables but especially onions that were often displayed in the local church, St. Augustine's of which he was a very strong supporter, acting as a church warden. Harold had two children, Jean and Alan. Alan followed his father onto the railway and was the third Gaythorpe generation to work on the Wensleydale line. Not only was his paternal grandfather a railwayman, so was his maternal grandfather and two of his uncles were signalmen. All in all six Gaythorpes were employed on the railways.

Signalman Harold Gaythorpe with help from his pet dog Midge opening the gates for a train and closing them to road traffic on the A1 road at Leeming Bar. c1957. Note the ship type wheel for opening and closing the gates.

Alan Gaythorpe Fireman/Engine driver.

Alan the son of Harold, started work in 1945 as a Lad Porter which meant him being a general hand who did all manner of tasks including the carrying of messages to the main signal box and eventually to keeping the trains times' logbook up to date. He then moved to the sheds at Northallerton where he became an engine cleaner and also was trained in the art of firing a locomotive. He left Northallerton and moved to Leyburn station as a fireman and it was while he was there that he met Kathleen Lloyd his future wife.

Alan starkly recalls the art of lighting the fire of a loco while at Leyburn. Lighting a fire in the fire-box of a loco was not just a case of lighting it and 'away we go' it was quite a complicated affair and not always successful. A layer of coal had to be placed evenly around the fire-box with a gap left in the centre where the fire lighters would have to be carefully laid. The wick of a paraffin 'goose-neck' was then lit which in turn ignited the fire lighters, which in turn supplied sufficient heat to set fire to the coal. It was without doubt a filthy job as initially the smoke did not go up the funnel as normal but escaped via the cab of the footplate leaving the fireman covered in soot.

Alan eventually became a full time fireman on the line and his regular driver was Johnny Watson, but he also fired for other drivers. While Alan was learning the job, his railway career was interrupted by the call of National Service. This was a chance for Alan to see the world. He entered the RAF and was posted to RAF Leeming just half a mile from his front door. He did not have a great need for the four rail warrants granted to all servicemen. He says he enjoyed his time [eighteen months] there and spent almost all of his off duty at home.

Alan and Johnny Watson at Northallerton station with Fred Sharpe their guard for the trip Garsdale.

In 1954 the passenger service ceased on the branch line on which he was the fireman on the last train to carry passengers. Not the train that ran with all the pomp and fanfare on the 24th April 1954, but the 9.05pm that ran from Northallerton as far as Leyburn. The next day he 'fired' the lowly milk cum passenger train that ran as normal the following day, which was truly the last train to carry people on the line.

In 1955, Alan was transferred to Newport sheds at Thornaby, where he carried on firing until 1970 after which he qualified to be a driver, not of steam but of the new diesels engines that were coming into service. Like Maurice Weighell and George Catchpole, when it came to steam versus diesel, it was no contest. Driving a diesel with all its comforts and cleanliness to say nothing of the efficiency was preferable to driving the smoky locomotives. However they all retained a soft spot for the old smokers. Alan drove engines to many parts of the north and north east and he even had his share of collecting a train of hoppers full of Redmire stone. Each driver from Thornaby worked the Redmire run one week in twenty four. For Alan it was a pleasant and nostalgic change. In 1992 he drove a stone train while Mr. Frank Mallon videoed the entire journey through the cab window. Alan was also at the controls of one of three passenger specials that marked the final closure of the line. He took early retirement in 1992 and went to live with Kathleen near Acklam.

Alan Gaythorpe died on the 13th July 2002.

Johnny and Alan in the usual G5 at Hawes with Jack Iveson platelayer.

At Garsdale- the most westerly point of the line.

Catchpole Country

George Catchpole Snr. Wagon Inspector

George Catchpole hailed from West Hartlepool but after he married in 1913 moved to Northallerton station. Eventually the couple had seven children, four boys and three girls. Three of the boys Walter [Bill] and Frank and George were to follow their father onto the railway. George made steady promotion to become a wagon inspector and covered the Northallerton-Cowton/Picton/Newby Wiske/Otterington of the main line and Hawes sections of the Wensleydale line.

Bill Catchpole. Shunter/Guard

Bill Catchpole was one of the most well known and popular characters of the former Wensleydale Railway in recent times. He was born in 1914 and although christened Walter, he was for some obscure reason always known as Bill. As was the norm in those days, son followed into his father's trade or calling and in 1931 Bill started work on the Wensleydale line. Less than one year later he had been made redundant due to the economic depression that beset the country in the 1930s. He found employment working at Castle Hill Farm when Harry Carter offered him a job with a pay packet of 16/- per week plus his food which for the times was fortune and feast. He toiled on the farm for four years until the call of the railway drew him back as a lad porter at Leyburn and Hawes stations. After a short while he progressed to the role of shunter on the branch line at Northallerton but in 1940 he changed tack to working as a guard. Bill worked with all the Weighells from Grandfather Weighell to Maurice the last of the railway Weighells.

In 1938 Bill's sister Grace married a regular soldier Don Allan and after war service he trained to be a signalman and acted as relief on the Wensleydale and Darlington lines. They set up home in a railway cottage at Jervaulx [which some railway men rudely pronounced as Jervolocks] When Grace's two brothers Bill and George travelled the line, they would often stop and beg a cup of tea from her while Bill would scrounge bacon and eggs which he would cook on the pan-shovel in the firebox of the engine after they had reached Leyburn. As a thank you, they would often heave a giant sized piece of coal onto the track side so that Grace and Don could keep their home fire burning.

Bill remembers the bitter winter of 1947 and 1962-63 when the Dales were cut off by huge snow drifts leaving many villages and farms isolated. Snow ploughs fitted to the front of engines were utilised to clear the snow along the lines and on several occasions the snow was so thick and heavy that the shear volume of it, either lifted the engine up or pushed it off the track. The drifting snow was so deep the crews of the engines could not see out of their cabs due to the wall of snow.

A snow plough train at Askrigg in 1963.

It is fairly well known that the men o' the line had ways and means of earning money other than through their railway jobs. Elsewhere in this book there are accounts of barbers' shops in signal cabins, knitting, vegetable gardening and the trapping of pheasants and rabbits. But there is one particular story that did the rounds which was told to the Northern Echo reporter Mike Amos aka John North in 1978 by Bill and others and was about another private enterprise scheme amongst the trains' crews. Rumour had it that they provided a private carrying service by delivering eggs, milk and sometimes pheasants to and from the farmsteads in the locality all for a nominal fee. One signalman, Ned Hartley even had a small bore shotgun in his cabin from which he would take pot shots at the scores of rabbits hopping near the cabin. Apparently those creatures tasted of the garlic that grew profusely in the woods around Constable Burton. Strange as it may seem those stories cannot be confirmed? Bill was not averse to catching rabbits along the line or the occasional hare of which he either sold or gave away. These money making pastimes were all part and parcel of the culture of the country railwayman everywhere.

Bill Catchpole retired from railway duties in December 1979 only to be called back to work again one week later as a checker on the stone trains that were coming out of Redmire. He would catch the train at Low Gates in Northallerton and travel to Redmire to begin his tour of duty. His skills and know how had been very much missed since his departure, especially when the quarries began producing ever larger quantities of stone. A typical day for him was to shunt six oil tankers off at Bedale, three trucks of coal for Leyburn and a 'rake' of the new British Steel wagons. Four years after being called back to work, Bill retired for the last time after serving for fifty one years. He then lived a quiet life hunting for rabbits with his 'team' of ferrets and having an occasional flutter on the horses.
Bill Catchpole died on the 1st of July 2002.

George Catchpole. Fireman/Engine driver

George Catchpole was the younger brother of Bill Catchpole and he started life as a Lad Porter at Northallerton in July 1937. Previous to joining the railway, he had been an apprenticed bricklayer to Stockdale's builders for 6/5d per week. His wage when starting with the railway was £1per week a princely sum to a seventeen year old lad. After the usual spell as Lad Porter he was moved to the position of engine cleaner and moved to Darlington. The move meant he had to take digs in the town and found himself sharing the digs with another railway lad at 63 Eastbourne Road. His tasks at the engine sheds were quite varied, among which he had to oil the big ends and straps [eccentric rods] of the engines over a huge pit or sometimes where ever the engine was in situ. Cleaning out the clinker of the engines was a dirty and tiresome job and on occasions George would actually climb inside the fire box to reach the cinders, but adds that in those days he was a slender lad weighing a mere eight stones. After a short while he was qualified as a 'passed cleaner' and the next move was to qualify as a 'passed fireman'. As described earlier, learning the art of firing was done by watching and listening to a qualified driver on the footplate. When he was assessed as being competent he would fill in any vacancies whenever a regular fireman was on holiday or was sick. If one was sent with a helpful driver, the learning was much easier, but sometimes a driver would deem it above his station to be too friendly to a young lad on the footplate. Generally speaking most drivers were quite helpful and friendly. George's next move was as regular fireman at Leyburn station on the Wensleydale branch and once more he had to find digs. He moved his meagre belongings to the home of Miss Blenkinsop and her brother who owned a house near the police station. Being the new lad, George was given the task of firing up the first train of the day, the 7.20am to Northallerton. However that meant having to arrive at the station by 4.am to begin the long drawn out rigmarole of lighting the fire in the engine. Lighting the fire was

in many ways almost as bad as cleaning out the firebox. In the shed at Leyburn there used to be an all night furnace which was an absolute boon for fire lighters such as George. On arriving he would go to the furnace and carry several shovels full of red hot cinders and place them into the boiler of the engine ensuring that the cinders sloped downwards to the boiler.

Using the standard fire lighters, a reasonable fire could be ignited in a fairly short time. Once a few pounds of steam pressure had been generated the release of the steam would create a venturi effect and draw air into the boiler causing the fire to increase in temperature which produced a good working head of steam. Although George became quite expert at fire lighting, lighting the fire on a Monday was always the most difficult. On a mid week day, the fire box of the engine was usually still warm from the previous day's labours and the lighting was relatively simple. On Monday mornings the engine fire box was as cold as a witch's heart and coupled with the possibility of the furnace in the shed being almost out, the Monday lighting was decidedly awkward, especially during a bitter Dales winter. One deep winter's snow during the war, George had managed to catch the local bus which should have taken him to Leyburn for him to start his shift. When the bus arrived at Bedale, the driver decided that the snow was too deep for him to drive to Leyburn and promptly turned round and left. It was 8pm and very dark and very cold. Without thinking twice, George accompanied by a postman simply set off and walked to Leyburn. [He says that is what was expected and the trains had to be fired.] He arrived in Leyburn and midnight extremely cold but well despite that fact that the local dairy wagon driver passed him and his companion on the road. For some reason he was paid a full days pay due to a mix up in accounts.

George quickly came to grips with the job of fireman and was soon a regular on the line. He recalls the problems sometimes encountered when entering tunnels especially the elongated ones. On many occasions the cab of the engine would fill with smoke despite there being funnels built into the tunnel roof. Some lines although not the Wensleydale the engines were fitted with breathing tubes for the crew to be able to inhale clear air. Another problem was what he describes as bad tracks. These were parts of the track that for some reason made the engine lurch and rattle uncomfortably. The rapid and sudden movements of the engine made it difficult to place the coal in the fire box. George said he often missed the box and on one occasion hit the driver with the blade of the shovel. Fortunately, the driver was wearing Long Johns as a precaution against the cold weather and came to no harm. George also wore Long Johns and more so when he transferred to the diesel engines. He says at least you had the warmth of the fire on a steamer, but the diesel although it had electrical heating, it was more often than not unserviceable and the system defeated the electricians at the sheds.

Like all railway systems, the branch lines carried war material to the many secluded military outposts, during the Second World War. Such traffic increased a thousand fold as military bases opened in almost every part of the country. The Wensleydale line was utilised in the movement of army spares, aircraft spares [for RAF Leeming] and military personnel. It was also used to move vast amounts of ammunition to various places within its delivery points. In late 1944 George was the fireman on an ammo train travelling from

Northallerton to Leyburn and on arriving at Bedale in the dark of an autumn night, they had to make a series of shunts into a siding for which the driver [who will remain anonymous] took charge. He suggested that George go off into Bedale and buy 'fish and chips twice' while he did the manoeuvring and that he would give a blast on the whistle when he was ready to go. George set off in search of their supper but when he got to the shop there was a long queue waiting and so he turned to make his way back to the engine. In the meantime, the driver had performed the shunts with his usual hard braking resulting in the ammunition wagons that were loose coupled, [unconnected save for a drawbar which was allowable due to the down gradient] kept the wagons pushing close up to the engine. The driver then pulled away rapidly and shunted the engine into a siding. The draw bar broke and unbeknown to the driver, the wagons began free wheeling down the gradient in the direction of Bedale station. By this time George who had arrived back at station, saw the wagons gathering speed toward the station. At that he ran full tilt to get back onto the engine. On the footplate the driver still unaware of the unfolding drama, was growing impatient with George's tardiness and blew a long blast on the whistle which was meant to say 'Hurry up!' The blast on the whistle attracted the attention of Mr. Plummer the Station Master who had spotted the ammunition wagons rumbling toward the station and with great presence of mind shouted to the crossing gateman to open the gates. The gateman speedily closed the gates to road traffic allowing the wagons to pass through safely. The wagons carried on their way until the opposite gradient brought them to a halt at which the brakes were pinned and the engine reconnected. Mr. Plummer was full of praise for the driver in his giving of a long blast on his whistle thus alerting everyone at the station. He declared that through his quick thinking the driver had saved Bedale town from a greater catastrophe than the one that Catterick had suffered earlier in the year when an ammunition train had exploded killing many people including the station master. George and especially the driver kept their counsel and took charge of the errant wagons and finished their shift deep in their own thoughts.

Another incident that has stayed with George happened during the war when he witnessed an attack by a German bomber that was ranging around the line in the Danby Wiske area. At the time he was working in the sheds at Northallerton when he heard the noise of an aircraft that was flying very low. He looked out and saw a twin engined bomber with crosses on its wings diving parallel with the railway lines. The gunner in the nose opened fire with his machine guns, at which George dived under a wagon full of coal. He reasoned that the bullets wouldn't penetrate the packed coal if any of them hit. The attack which was a target of opportunity raid lasted just a few seconds and then it was all over. For a young seventeen year old it was quite a frightening experience. Another experience but more of the humourous side, was when he was firing on a W.D. War 'Austerity' engine. These 2-8-0 or 2-10-0 Khaki painted engines were heavy and rugged engines and weighed in at 78.3 tons, were built for the War Department for work with goods trains but never with passengers. They were normally based at Thornaby but occasionally were used on the Redmire run for hauling the dust trains from Redmire. This is George's somewhat pithy description of the occupational hazards of firing aboard the Austerities. "Keeping the fire going on the W.D. could be an awkward task at times as they had a very large tender and fire box. The fire box was designed to take very large pieces of coal and had a long hinged swing type door and when opened, the heat was quite overwhelming, so when you turned and bent down to get another shovel of coal, it burnt your arse!"

A 2-8-0 WD 'Austerity'
at Wensley

George at the controls of a
Bo Bo type 2D which had a
Swiss Sulzer engine
with Alwyn Thompson
and Dick Pashby.
This double cabbed ended diesel
sported the luxury
of having a kitchen galley
in each cab.

His experiences of the dangers and inconveniences of railway life continued when he was firing for Bill Stephenson on a J.25 on the Hawes goods run. They were stopped in Bedale station when a Tees-side to Redmire J.27 steamer returning from Redmire with a load of stone, ran into difficulties. The brake pin on the J.27 had broken which resulted in the engine brakes failing. The crew tried desperately to slow down the train that was on the down bank run into Bedale. They stayed with it and as a last resort they put the engine in reverse which had the effect of retarding the train somewhat and then 'baled' out and ran to make an emergency call by telephone to Bedale. When they got the message, George and his driver endeavoured to shunt their train into a siding. There was not quite enough space for the entire length of the train and the runaway train came rolling into Bedale station [gates closed to road traffic] and clipped the rear of their guard's van. Fortunately no real damage was sustained, but the runaway train's engine happened to touch the signal cabin, physically moving it a couple of inches to one side. Such are the potential and actual dangers of working on the railway.

After the war George advanced from fireman to driver [but not before failing his first driving examination] and on many occasions he had as his guard, his older brother Bill. To complete the family railway work ethos, they would often meet up with their father who was a wagons inspector and their sister Grace who lived with her signalman husband at Jervaulx, would meet up at Redmire. The three male family members worked the Wensleydale line for many years and for that reason and with having a sister and brother in law involved it was known quite fittingly as 'Catchpole Country'.

After a short while driving the steam engines, George transferred to the new diesel engines and often ran the Northallerton to Harrogate service and also the Teesside passenger services. Like Alan Gaythorpe he much preferred the quietness and clean efficiency of the diesel engine, not withstanding the poor heaters, as against the uncomfortable smoky and dirty steamers, but he still has a soft spot for those amiable puffers that plied between Northallerton and Hawes. In his final days with B.R George took charge of a passenger train from York to Northallerton which was routed via Starbeck in Harrogate due to a collision near Thirsk.

In 1968 George was made redundant and eventually left the railway to work at the York Trailer factory in Northallerton finally retiring in 1987.

N.B. There was another Catchpole railwayman and he was Frank, the youngest member of the family. Frank didn't work on the Wensleydale but worked on the Darlington line as a signalman. Frank volunteered for the army in 1939 and was sent to France with the BEF where he was killed in the fighting rearguard action at Dunkirk. He lies buried at the Commonwealth War Grave Cemetery near Neuport in Belgium.

The Engine Driver

Although engine drivers are previously featured, it is only right that a veteran driver of the branch should be featured individually.

Laurie Atkinson; Engine driver.

 Laurie Atkinson began his career on the Wensleydale line in the early 1930s and made the usual progress from passed fireman till finally qualifying as an engine driver. Laurie says that, to him it was just a job and his forty plus years on the line [minus five years in the army] were ordinary but he does recall some memories. Once when taking a passenger train from Hawes to Northallerton, they were held up between Jervaulx and Crakehall by a donkey that was strolling down the centre of the track. No amount of shooing and threats would make it move off the line, so Laurie had no other course but to travel at the ambling speed of the jackass. The second event was much more serious. Once while taking his engine on the Bedale-Crakehall stretch his engine collided with a tractor that had stalled on the amenity crossing between the two stations. The tractor's wheels had begun to slip and skid on the wooden sleepers at which the driver leapt from the vehicle and made a run for it when he saw the approaching train. Although travelling at a very low speed there was no time to stop as the tractor was obscured by trees on a relatively sharp bend. The tractor was severely damaged in the collision but the engine was barely scratched. Fortunately the driver of the tractor was not injured and the event was settled amicably.

The third event was a most enjoyable affair and with it came a modicum of kudos. One day when arriving for work at Northallerton station, Laurie was approached by a rather anxious looking station master who was in need of an engine driver. He asked Laurie if he would act as conductor for an E.P [Express Passenger] train that was standing at the station's mainline platform. In railway parlance, a conductor was a qualified driver who was charged with accompanying a regular driver of a train when there was to be a change of route. This particular express had arrived in the station from Newcastle and before it could set off, it was discovered that there were problems with the signal lights on the route to York. This meant the express had to be re-routed via Ripon and [Starbeck] Harrogate. The regular driver was not familiar with it so he by regulation was not allowed to drive unaccompanied. Laurie climbed onto the footplate and made ready for the journey.

To his surprise the regular driver of the express informed Laurie that he had been driving for his allotted time and was due for a break and promptly disappeared into the comfort of the train to have his bait [sandwiches] and indicated that Laurie should drive the express to York. Although the conductor was ostensibly there to guide the driver through the unknown route, in reality the driver usually let his conductor do the driving while he stood back. Laurie took over the controls and duly delivered the passenger express to York. As he climbed off the footplate he glanced along the side of the engine to check which express he had been driving and it turned out to be the world famous record breaking MALLARD! Although Laurie is a modest man, he was secretly pleased with that 'out of the blue' chance to drive one of the most famous if not the most famous streamlined steam engine in the world.

After years of driving the small steam engines along the Wensleydale line, Laurie Atkinson was given the opportunity to drive this classic steam engine, the record breaking Mallard

The Wensleydale Rainbows

Artie Rainbow; Platelayer.

 Arthur Rainbow was one of a family of plate laying railwaymen. His father Arthur Robinson Rainbow began work as a platelayer on the Wensleydale line in the summer of 1912. In 1949 he retired early due to injury and the young Arthur left the farm on which he was employed and took over the vacant position. Artie as he was known began working on the line in early 1950 track-walking the Jervaulx-Bedale section of the line. Although used to hard work, at times being a platelayer was as equally hard if not harder than working on the farm and he most certainly walked many more miles than he ever did on the farm. He worked alongside such characters as George Parsley and Harry Hartley, two stalwarts of the line and learnt many skills from those two men.

Artie never regretted working on the railway especially when he and a number of fellow platelayers were invited to rail conventions organised by the National Union of Railwaymen and their continental counterparts. The trips were designed to show British railwaymen the working practices and systems of European railways. The countries visited were, Holland, Austria, Germany, Switzerland, France and Ireland. With a smile of satisfaction, Artie relishes the thought that those trips did not cost him or his colleagues a single penny save for personal expenses, as all accommodation from the hotels to the mode of travel was first class. They were given strict instructions not to let their time away 'working' on the Continent to be taken out of their annual holiday allowance.

Diminutive Artie Rainbow was a very skilled and adaptable platelayer and although not the biggest or tallest of men, he was equal to anyone along the tracks of Wensleydale when it came down to doing the job. This skill and ability showed with his winning of three British Railways Awards for consistently high quality track work. He retired in 1982 and now lives a quite life in his cottage at Crakehall.

Until recent years he toured the USA and Canada with a like minded pal. Artie had two brothers, Ronald and Walter who for a short time also worked as platelayers on the same section of line so completing the line up of the 'Four Rainbows' of Wensleydale'.

BRITISH RAILWAYS
NORTH EASTERN REGION

THIS IS TO CERTIFY THAT
A. RAINBOW
WAS A LENGTHMAN IN
JERVAULX LENGTH
WHICH WAS AWARDED THE
PRIZE FOR HIGH STANDARD
OF PERMANENT WAY
MAINTENANCE ON THE
CLASS "D" LINES OF THE
DARLINGTON
DISTRICT IN 1960

....
DISTRICT ENGINEER

....
CHIEF CIVIL ENGINEER

One of three certificates awarded to Artie Rainbow for his high quality track work

The

Wensleydale

Railway

in

Colour

The Walls family at Aysgarth station c1912. George Walls was the Station Master, was the son of the Station Master who held office at Potto near Stokesley.
There are very strong railway connections amongst the wider Walls family.

Bedale Station

Bedale

*The Queen Mother greeting
the crowd with a regal wave.*

*The Queen Mother
with the
Chief Constable
of North Yorkshire
during her visit
to Bedale.*

*The Royal Train
on the platform*

The photogenic and ubiquitous 'K1 Mogul' 62005 heading up a Type 2 Bo-Bo diesel as it approaches Bedale crossing on 20th May 1967. The Mogul was on a Dales Tour and was the last steam train to run to and from Redmire.

Mogul passing through the gates...

...and passing into the platform

*Alan
Gaythorpe
stops to
allow Bill
Chadd to
board
Gartosh
Pathfinder at
Leeming Bar.*

*Alan and Bill
Chadd with a
trackman at
Leeming Bar.*

*Alan Gaythorpe
at the controls
of Pathfinder.*

*Running into the
curve of
Bedale station.*

*Through the
windscreen.
A posse of
enthusiasts greets
Pathfinder as it
approaches
Crakehall station.*

*A diesel
stone train
at Redmire*

Bill Catchpole showing off a hare snared on line side at Wensley.

A smiling Bill in the cab.

Closing the gates at Wensley

A classic shot of one of the last stone trains as it meanders its way out of Redmire.

Overturned stone hoppers at Bedale after the accident of December1988

A British Rail crane clearing away the debris after the accident.

The telephone from the office at Bedale Station.

Alan Hiscock sitting at his desk in Northallerton main line signal box. The Wensleydale loop can be seen at the bottom of the board.

Northallerton main line signal box. Once the most advanced signal box in the UK but now gone for ever.

The clock used in Bedale Station office

The WRA in Colour

Two WRA enthusiasts standing outside the Portico at Leeming Bar during the first summer of the opening of the shop and the introduction of Pilgrim.

Inside the Leeming Bar shop.

Michael Bentley and Arthur Hartley in the Leyburn shop

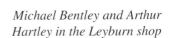

The Buffet car at Leeming Bar

*Olive Mahoney serving
at the buffet counter*

Looking down to the buffet diner

*Rolling stock
at Leeming Bar*

*Rolling stock acquired
by the Association*

*Michael Bentley with WRA Patron
Robert Hardy standing next to the
Wensleydale Railway
Reliant 'Vantique'*

*The pay kiosk for
Pilgrim travellers*

*David Lee
on the 'footplate' of Pilgrim.
Driving the little steamer is a
change from one his earlier steeds,
for David is a former
Vulcan bomber pilot.*

*Pilgrim Drivers
David Lee and John Hardcastle*

Colin Cooper standing next to a display at the WRA summer exhibition in Northallerton Town Hall 2002.

The 'Whistle Stop' kiosk at Northallerton station. Volunteer Audrey Heathcote serves a customer prior to him boarding the 9.40am train for London.

The mile of track dedication at Hawes. by Railtrack

Although the Dales National Park saddle tank engine positioned at Hawes station is not part of the WR set up, it adds ambience to the history and heritage of the line.

The Motor Driver

By any definition, railways are about locomotives, rolling stock, lines, signal boxes, freight and passengers and the Wensleydale branch line was no different. However, there was another business common to all railways and in particular to the Wensleydale branch line which, by and large has gone unnoticed since those heady days of the rail traffic, and that is the road freight division. The official name given to the road freight division of the railway was the Road Motor Department which came under the auspices of the rather grandly named Central Road Motor Services York. Until the rapid expansion of private road delivered freight and parcels, the railways of the UK had a very busy and diverse motor transport fleet that delivered almost any type of goods, from private parcels to aeroplane engines. In common with all railway lines, there were a great number of men employed as lorry and van drivers. In the very early days, goods were delivered by horse and cart but very soon the ubiquitous motor lorry replaced the plodding but reliable horses.

Herbert Jobling with his Fordson lorry c 1947. We will ignore the condition of the tyres and unusual size of headlights and sidelights

The Yorkshires Dales are nothing if not a diverse agricultural landscape with many scores of cattle and sheep farms scattered around its rolling hills and valleys. Because of those farms, animal feed delivery became one of the many sources of income for the Railways via the Road Motor Dept. Contracts were made for the storing and selling by such companies as Silcocks and Levers [with agents taking the orders] with dozens of lorries ranging all around the Dales delivering tons of animal food. As important as the animal feeds were, the delivery of a whole range of goods and private household parcels to local shops and warehouses was also another service. Although the goods delivery division is largely forgotten, the memory of the goods and parcel lorry with its peaked capped driver meandering through market towns such as Leyburn, Middleham and Hawes and many other villages and hamlets, is indelibly written in the minds of many people of the Dales. There follows the story of one character who worked for the Leyburn Motor Dept.

Jack Dent motor mechanic.

Jack Dent began his apprenticeship in 1941 in the motor dept at Leyburn and when he was well into his seventies; his memories were crystal clear of his early days as a junior motor mechanic there. His immediate boss at the garage was the fitter in charge Charles Clarkson, but in charge overall there was Bill Newstead a Grade 1 fitter and another apprentice Ted Dawson. Jack's senior boss at Leyburn was Station Master Mr. Mattison. The motor drivers based within the working area of Leyburn depot and Leeming Bar to Askrigg were, Harry Boddy, Morley Ward, Jim Peacock, Bob Keyes, Mr. Bailey, Eric Janney, Mr. Harrison, Norman Carr, Dick Davison and Bobby Pearson. The fleet of lorries serving the line was a mix of Fordson 3 tonners, a Ford Thames and a Bedford diesel which was used exclusively for milk collection. There was also a very old Thornycroft lorry which was chronically underpowered and extremely unpopular with the drivers. Fixing and mending those lorries was Jack's main task which meant a regular decarbonising of engines, or a decoking as he called it. A slow and laborious task which might puzzle some of today's mechanics. At the Leyburn depot, the mechanics also stripped back axles and fitted new crown wheels and pinions, changed half shafts and universal joints, plus the usual run o' the mill mending of mud guards and flooring. To name a few of the motley set of tools at Jack's disposal while at Leyburn, there were, 1 welding set with 1 torch and 3 nozzles. 1[very heavy] electric drill which had LNER 1918 stamped on its side, an assortment of saws and spanners and a partially bald wire brush. However Jack had another job which happened only on the first working day of the New Year, and was one he enjoyed immensely. He would board a train at Leyburn and travel up and down the line between Hawes and Leeming Bar fixing new road tax discs on all vehicles with strict instructions to bring back the old discs as proof that the new ones had been issued to the correct vehicles. Once he was established in that job, one of the engine drivers, Mr. Ken Brown used to allow Jack to ride on the footplate and to fire the engine. On more than one occasion Jack was left to drive the engine [oh so slowly] while the proper driver and the fireman walked alongside checking their rabbit snares; a minor money making pastime on the Wensleydale line.

If the goods drivers and their lorries have been all but forgotten, another branch of that service is virtually unknown, and that branch is the Horse Box Service. The small market town of Middleham is by far the hub of racehorse training in the North of England. Although racing stables are scattered far and wide, there were only two Horse Box service stations for the whole country and they were at Leyburn and Malton. Wensleydale was and still is rich in the history of the Sport of Kings, having several successful trainers and training stables. To name but a few, there was, Dobson Peacock, father of Harry and Matt Peacock, Sam Hall, Harry Blackshaw, the redoubtable Captain Neville Crump, and currently Mark Johnston who runs a string at Middleham, and by the year of 2002, had become the top trainer in the UK earning more than £3m in prize money.

In the hey day of the Horse Box service, there was at Leyburn station yard, a large wooden garage that housed four Albion and one Gilford horse boxes. In those early days the racing trainers didn't own private boxes and so utilised the horse box service provided by the railway companies and special horse box carriages on the trains. On race days, four horse box specialist drivers, namely, Harry Boddy, Jim Peacock, Bob Keyes and Mr. Bailey would eschew their workaday uniforms and don a smart double breasted barrathea uniform replete with gold buttons and a

chauffeur's type peaked cap. They had to look the part as they might be in the presence of dukes, lords and knights to say nothing of Royalty at the many race meetings of the Sport of Kings. [Eventually this smart uniform succumbed to overuse and became crumpled and rather dusty and was hardly distinguishable from their ordinary working clothes.]

There were a number of winners of classic races that had been trained in Middleham and perhaps the most famous being Dante the winner of the Epsom Derby in 1945, trained by Matt Peacock, owned by Sir Eric Ohlson and ridden by Billy Nevett. No doubt followers of the steeplechase variety of horseracing would argue that Sheila's Cottage, Teal and Merryman all winners of the Grand National were the most famous. Whichever, those horses showed that the trainers and jockeys from the North Riding of Yorkshire were among the best.

Jack Dent left Leyburn in 1948 as a fully qualified motor mechanic. After retirement he became an unpublished author and even wrote his biography and was featured in a popular week end newspaper when he was almost swept away by flood water near his home town of Leeds. However his greatest personal achievement was learning to fly and pilot his own aircraft, which was a long way from driving and working on those rickety old motor lorries of Wensleydale. He even survived a forced landing in a farmer's field much to the dismay of his passenger and wife, Mrs Pat Dent.
Jack Dent died in July 2001.

The Horse Box Era

Dante the 1945 winner of the Derby being led into his horsebox at Leyburn, Mr Stephenson the Station Master and Harry Boddy look on while Chris King takes the horses head.

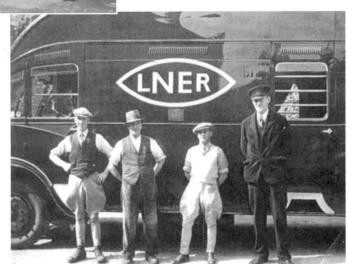

Stable lads Chris King and Swank Smith, the winning jockey Billy Nevett and driver Harry Boddy. Mr. Smith was given the sobriquet of 'Swank' due to his flashy style of speech and because he was a Londoner.

The bosses. Rail official, Sir Eric Ohlson, Owner. Matt Peacock, trainer, Rail official. The plaque on the side of the horsebox bears the inscription DANTE Sir Eric Ohlson's Colt Trained by Mr. M.J. Peacock Travelled in this vehicle from Middleham to Newmarket and back to win THE DERBY 1945

Sheila's Cottage the winner of the Grand National 1952 being led out of the LNER horse box.

I would like to thank Ursula Jackson for her efforts in acquiring the photographs of the horse boxes via friends and the names of the people featured on them, especially the names of the staff from Middleham stables.

Tony Eaton. Motor driver.

I vividly recall an incident while working out of Leyburn as a relief motor lorry driver in 1960. The previous year I had been demobbed from the RAF and had taken a job as a motor driver at the North End Goods Yard in Northallerton. While on relief duties on the Wensleydale line, I was required to catch the early morning goods [steam] train from Northallerton to Leyburn where I was expected to deliver parcels, goods and the almost obligatory Silcocks and Levers animal feed to the village folk and farmers of Wensleydale. I choose the word expected, as I hadn't so much as paid a fleeting visit to the area in my whole life, so needless to say I became somewhat disoriented and perplexed driving among and through the many small roads in the valleys of the dales, visiting abodes with such strange names as Unthank Farm and any number of Gills. I think the somewhat impenetrable dialect of Dales-speak by the locals was part of the problem for this lad from Lincolnshire. On one occasion, such was my frustration at not being able to find some lonely outposts of farms and sleepy hamlets whose names were a mystery to me, I returned to Leyburn with six parcels [out of sixty] undelivered. This did not suit the resident goods clerk there; the redoubtable Sheila Houseman, who let me know in her own inimitable way that it wasn't good enough. My 'crime' was soon forgotten but she always strove to keep the parcels delivery service efficient. For my part I regretted it, but time had been running out and I did have a train to catch. I endeavoured to make up the late deliveries the next day, which I succeeded in doing. Having that particular parcels run, was one way of learning one's way around those beautiful Dales and in many ways it was a most enjoyable way of doing so.

The Goods Clerk

Sheila Houseman. Clerk

Sheila Houseman [nee Garnett] was born in Leyburn and was the daughter of a local coal agent. Sadly her father died at an early age and Sheila was required to get a job to help her widowed mother. She applied for a job with British Railways and in 1951 began life on the Wensleydale line as a 16 year old junior booking office clerk at Leyburn station fresh out of school. She arrived at work on her brand new Hercules bicycle and said that when she reported to the Leyburn booking office she 'felt every part of a schoolgirl in her herringbone tweed suit

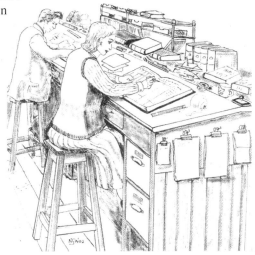

and knee socks'. Almost immediately she was being taught how to book and record parcels traffic, all done in her own very neat hand writing. Within a very short time Sheila literally blotted her copy book when she knocked a bottle of ink over two pages of the entry ledger. She recalled one comical scene when a porter asked her to keep an eye on a greyhound passenger that had been left unattended on the platform. Before Sheila could comply with the request the dog took off at high speed and raced past the porter who let out a most memorable cry, 'Stop that dog, it's a parcel!'

Three years later she witnessed the closure of the passenger service and the end of 'Old Faithful' on the Wensleydale line, but the station remained open for the goods service trains that still ran. In 1956 she married Wilf Houseman who was a signalman on the line. Ten years after the loss of the passenger services, the Beeching report gave the axe to the goods service and like many stations on the line, Leyburn closed for good. Sheila was transferred to Catterick station on the Richmond line and then in 1968 she arrived at Northallerton station where she ended her 42 year career with the railway. While at Northallerton Sheila and Wilf and two other railwaymen Norman Coverdale and Les Collins developed the stunning garden display at Northallerton station by growing more than 4,000 summer bedding plants.

Long into her retirement she still kept up her keen interest in gardening.

Sheila Houseman passed away in August 2002.

Kathleen Gaythorpe. Clerk

Kathleen Gaythorpe [nee Lloyd] began her career on the railway as a clerk at Leyburn station. She recalls her first week at Leyburn station when she fell foul of that fiery race horse trainer, Captain Neville Crump. Captain Crump was renowned for his short temper and disposition for not suffering fools gladly. One of his more genteel but comical idiosyncrasies was when ever he was out riding through Middleham village of an early morning;

he was wont to shout, Tally Ho! Get up you lazy buggers! Clearly he was a man not to be crossed, but Kathleen did just that. During that first and slightly confusing week in the booking office, the Captain was expecting to take delivery of a racehorse at his stables that was being brought in a horsebox from Northallerton via Leyburn. In the event there was a monumental mix up. Kathleen whose job it was to administer the paperwork, ended up by sending a yearling that should have gone to the Peacock stables near Richmond, to the Crump stables instead with the race horse ending up in Richmond. So in her first working week at Leyburn, she received a high decibel 'Crumpian' rollicking which she has never forgotten. She wasn't the first and most certainly was not the last to do so. As stated earlier it was at Leyburn where she met her husband-to be-Alan Gaythorpe. At the latter end of her time on the Wensleydale line, it fell to Kathleen to issue some of the last tickets on the day the passenger services ceased.

Leyburn clerical staff c. 1953
Elizabeth Clark, Mr. Stephenson,
Kathleen Lloyd, Jim Mason.

Travellers Tales

Over the years of its existence, the Wensleydale line employed many hundreds of men and women in a wide variety of jobs. Over that same span of time, the line carried many thousands of passengers and no story of the Wensleydale line would be complete without a sample of the experiences, trials and tribulations of travelling on that pastoral meandering railway in the Yorkshire Dales. For the fare paying passenger, almost all journeys by train are ordinary, bordering on the uninteresting. Occasionally however, an event sometimes overtakes them or an opportunity arises for them to be involved in the methods of railway work. Sadness and shock sometimes accompany those events as well as pleasure and memorable times. There follows a selection of tales related by different people who have good reason to remember the Wensleydale railway and those who worked the line.

We begin with a series of contemporary photographs.

Through the lens of
Jim Sedgewick

Jim Sedgewick of Danby Wiske.

Farmer Jim Sedgewick from Danby Wiske near Northallerton has been a keen local historian and railway buff for more than half a century. His interests are wide and varied and this interest shows in the vast number of artefacts and spectacular photographs of railways scenes that he has accrued over the years. Jim was always ready with his camera and was ever prepared to travel up and down the Wensleydale line in all weathers to capture forever that picture that tells a story in its own right. He says that he is no photographer, yet some of the following pictures are so distinctive and so full of interest, that the plea about his lack of skill doesn't arise. There follows more than a score of high class photographs taken between 1954 [the last passenger train] and 1959, of the many stations and crossing points of the Wensleydale line photographed by Jim over the past fifty years all complete with date and accurate caption.

Smoke & Steam

'twixt'

Garsdale

&

Northallerton

A delightful view of Garsdale station as the last passenger train J21 0-6-0 No 650338
'Old Faithful' sets out to Northallerton. The engine had just returned from the stockaded
turn-table at Garsdale. The second carriage down from the engine is a First Class
Plum & Spilt Milk* passenger carriage specially hired as a mobile pub by a
Mr. R. McCrombie-Metcalfe of Leyburn on which he and 42 friends drank several toasts
to the Wensleydale Railway line on the 24th April 1954.
Further down the line, a banner displayed the words.
'Death of a veteran-Old Faithful' Rest in Peace.
* This colour scheme was known colloquially as **Blood and Custard.**

The crowds awaiting the arrival of the
last train on the platform at Garsdale.
The figure 1st and 2nd from the right are
Paul Barraclough and David Tyreman,
Peter Blakey a long time member of the
WRA is 3rd from the right.

The engine arriving at the station.
George Ezzard the guard on the train is
standing on the right.

Old Faithful running around the last train in Garsdale station where eager passengers await to entrain. Waiting with them on the platform is the well known [at the time] BBC radio producer Barney Colehan who was one of the fare paying passengers. 24th April 1954

A steamer traversing Appersett Gill viaduct. Arguably one of the most eye catching and evocative sights on the Wensleydale line. The famous Boniface is seen pushing out plenty of steam as she climbs the 5 1/4 miles incline to Garsdale. 5th March 1959

The opposite view Loco 4F43913 drifting down the bank to a gloomy Moss Head Tunnel. 4th March 1959

Two K1 engines at Wensley. The one on the right is a mineral train from Wensley the one on the left is the Hawes goods train.

A K1 2-6-0 No 62003 entering Leyburn while on the Hawes goods run.
Originally there were two signal boxes at Leyburn, one east and one west with double lines.

A Wensley mineral train passing through Jervaulx. The effects of 'pinning down the brakes' can be seen at the curve of the wagons. This was an end of term special for the boys of Aysgarth Prep School which, rather quaintly, was situated in Newton le Willows.

A Saturday afternoon horsebox special passing through Leeming Bar.

A very smoky parcels train arriving at Bedale on the same day as the Leeming air show. [Note the curved platform] The porter pushing the trolley is Bob Mitchinson on relief duties from Northallerton

A six car diesel Special passing Ham Hall crossing heading for Leeming Bar. On the 20th of September 1958, Royal Air Force Leeming held an 'At Home Day' to celebrate the 18th anniversary of the Battle of Britain.
British Railways had laid on shuttle service of several six car diesel trains to convey passengers from the Tees-Side area for the show.

Passengers alighting at Leeming Bar station to await transport into Leeming aerodrome. Bill Hall was the signalman on duty for that day, and he had the most busiest of days in years. Apart from the RAF Leeming air show, passenger traffic and the horsebox and parcel trains, there were also several mineral trains to contend with. The constant closing of the gates to road traffic created long tail backs on the [A1] Great North Road.

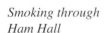

Smoking through Ham Hall

A signalman handing the single line tablet to the driver at Ainderby

A Damp and Dark Garsdale

The Duke of Edinburgh's A4 Special No. 60025 Falcon heading slowly through Northallerton West on the 15th November 1955 for an overnight stop. The Royal Special was pulled up the Hawes branch for breakfast. Engine K1 No 62044 supplied steam heat for the Royal train and can be seen in the distance.

The Northern Dales Tour. An A8 No. 69855 doubled with 62360 SLS with eight coaches, gaining speed after passing Yafforth Gates September 1955

The 'North Yorkshire' passing Northallerton west. 25th April 1964.

An almost invisible steam engine in the snow
passing Castle Hills, Northallerton

Maurice Simpson

Maurice Simpson is a retired farmer who lives in the village of Deighton some five miles from Northallerton. Although Maurice spent his working life on the farm, as a seventeen year old youth, he had for a short time an entirely illegal and nocturnal job as a fireman on the Wensleydale line. His father Wilfred was an engine driver of some experience who had worked in the North East and was one of the many drivers on the Northallerton to Hawes line. Wilf Simpson had many different firemen while on that line including the two most well known, the Weighell brothers, but on some occasions he had an unknown young man as his fireman, his son Maurice.

On many Saturdays in 1950, Maurice used to travel to Northallerton railway station where his father was due to take the later afternoon service train from Northallerton to Garsdale. Unseen by the stationmaster, or more to the point making sure that the stationmaster didn't see him; Maurice would slip into the cab of the loco and wait for the train to depart. Once the journey had got underway, the regular fireman would take over the driving of the train and Maurice would take over the task of the fireman. His father would then sit back, relax and enjoy the ride while Maurice shovelled on the coals and the fireman drove the engine. Maurice discovered that firing a locomotive engine wasn't simply a matter of shovelling on the coal and getting a red hot fire. He was taught to place the coal evenly into the four corners of the firebox by tilting the shovel so as to get an even burn which would keep up a working head of steam. He was told to keep a constant eye on the steam gauge and was shown the level of pressure required to keep the engine working. The job of firing was much harder and constant on the outward journey to Hawes and to Garsdale than it was on the return. The reason for this was that the line rose quite steeply, up to 750 feet above sea level as it entered the undulating tors and valleys of the Dales. The return trip was a case of almost freewheeling, as the downward gradient gave almost all the impetus required for the train to travel. On the way out and when they reached Leyburn, an order fish and chips 'four times' [this included one supper for the guard] from the local fish n' chip shop was made, and collected on the return trip.

Maurice 'got away' with his illicit job for many months but didn't receive so much as a single penny [from his father] for his efforts, nor did he expect to, he simply loved doing the job. Another small but important task he was given was the collection of the 'Tablets'. Tablets were large hoops of metal with wedges of lead attached, hence the name tablets which were delivered by hand to and from a signalman en route. This gave them priority on that stretch of line and allowed them to travel. Maurice also recalls other illicit practices by some of the chaps who worked the line. Some were known to leave the task of driving to the fireman and then go off to work in the fields for a local farmer, all done to earn an extra few shillings.

A farm on the move
The Northern Echo.

Lock stock and barrel.
Farming equipment moved by rail.

Railways have moved many varied and strange items in its history, but moving livestock, implements and wooden buildings of a farm must be a rare event. British Railways carried out such a task in 1952 when they moved Raymond Wilkinson's farm from Tees-side to Leeming Bar on the Wensleydale line.

Encroaching houses drive farmer away.

Mr. Raymond Wilkinson the tenant farmer at Berwick Hills Farm near Ormesby left Teesside by road with his wife and two young children for their new home at an 80 acre farm at Leeming Bar. His farming equipment and three horses were transported in a 19 wagon chartered train earlier in the day.

Land for housing.

In three years 200 acres of it had become part of the new Berwick Hills housing estate. The other 85 acres were to be used shortly for the same purpose" he added. So Mr. Wilkinson must go. But in moving he established a post-war record for British Railways at Middlesbrough. The train which carried his farming equipment including tractors, hay carts, hen houses and ploughs in the first 18 wagons, and the three shire horses in the final truck, was the first of its kind to leave the station since the war ended.

Cutting from the Northern Echo

Encroaching houses drive farmer away

THE development of Middlesbrough has driven a farmer away from the town and broken a 60-year-old family link with a 285-acre farm at Ormesby.

Mr. Raymond Wilkinson, the tenant farmer at Berwick Hill Farm, Ormesby, left Teesside by road yesterday with his wife and two young children to their new home at an 80-acre farm at Leeming Bar. His farming equipment and three horses were transported by rail in a 19-wagon chartered train earlier in the day.

Land for housing

Mr. Wilkinson told The Northern Echo: "I have had no choice but to leave my farm at Ormesby and buy another place where there is a future for me." The Ormesby farm had been farmed by his parents for 40 years and by himself for 4 years.

In three years 200 acres of it had become part of the new Berwick Hills housing estate. "The other 85 acres were to be used shortly for the same purpose," he added.

So Mr. Wilkinson must go. But, in moving, he established a post-war record for British Railways at Middlesbrough. The train which carried his farming equipment, including tractors, hay-carts, hen-houses and ploughs in the first 18 wagons, and the three horses in the final truck, was the first of its kind to leave the station since the war ended.

"The Wilkinson farm equipment arriving at Leeming Bar in 1952. Their three Shire horses being led off. L to r Jewel-Bonnie- Trixie

103

Two people who didn't actually use the branch line but who had dealings with it in a convoluted way were Peter and Joan Tarran. Peter and Joan bought by tender from British Rail in 1974, the property known as 1&2 Ainderby Gates through agents Willman Douglas & Gray. The two houses were originally occupied by a crossing gate keeper and a lengthman. Once in possession Joan and Peter spent long hours demolishing all outbuildings, i.e. wash house, coalhouse and earth closets and toiled for many months spending no small amount of money in converting it into a modern dwelling. After two years of back aching and some heart aching work living a mean life in a caravan on the site, they moved into what is now a very modern spacious and well appointed house. They are looking forward to the day when once again trains crowded with smiling passengers rumble past their back garden. With the acquisition of the property came a copy of the Deeds from the time when the land was purchased for the building of the rail line and the station house in 1840. Below are three samples of the contents of those Deeds.

Three samples of the Deeds now in the hands of the Tarrans.

Names from the Past

I am grateful to Mr. Edward Mason of Barnard Castle for his diligence and expertise in setting down his memories of his times travelling up and down the Wensleydale line, first as a schoolboy in the 1920s and 1930s then as an adult until its closure in 1954. Edward was born into a Wensleydale railway family and recalls with a great degree of accuracy some of the many characters and events of those times. He lists many of the people who worked on some of the stations he frequented, Leyburn, Askrigg, Aysgarth, Hawes and Wensley His description of the duties of the porter/signalmen makes for very interesting reading and the tasks expected of them is quite surprising.

Station Masters; Askrigg, Nelson Hutchinson, Aysgarth, Mr. Atkinson, Leyburn, Mr. Batty. Wensley and Constable Burton, Ernest Widdell.
Signalmen; Hawes, John 'Pasty' Mason [my uncle] Leyburn, James Mason [my father] Nessfield Hartley.
Engine drivers; Leyburn, Johnny Watson, Alf Brown, Tommy Briggs, Ernie Wade [Sentinel driver]
Platelayers; Leyburn, George Parsley, Wensley, Mr. Hutchinson.
Porters; Ike Wilkinson, Leyburn, Fred Sharp of Northallerton.
Horsebox drivers; Morley Ward, Harry Boddy, Jimmy Peacock.
Lorry driver Leyburn, George Lumley.
Booking Clerk; Bob Lambert.
Coal Agent; Bob Grainger.

As a young boy I lived in the station house at Wensley with my parents and two sisters. My father James Mason was a porter/signalman there from 1925 to 1935 when we moved to Leyburn for him to take up duties at Leyburn West box. However that box was closed in 1936 and all workings transferred to Leyburn East box. In the 1930s, the porter/signalman's duties at Wensley were shared by two employees, my father and Jack Richardson and those duties which were quite considerable, were as follows;

1. Ensuring the safe passage of trains by correct operation of the signals and points.
2. Operating the 'block' system which on a single track ensured that two trains would never be on the same piece of track.
3. Acting as booking clerk.
4. Acting as coal agent and operating the weigh-house across the coal yard. The coal was collected by horse and cart.
5. Acting as goods clerk.
6. Cleaning the station premises, i.e., the booking office, signal cabin, three waiting rooms, [one of which was Lord Bolton's private waiting room] station toilets, and the platform.
7. Keeping all fire fighting equipment in order.
8. Cleaning, trimming and filling the paraffin signal lamps and climbing up the signals to replace them every few days. [There was a small room called the 'Porter's Room' where the lamps were stored and cleaned and it always smelt of paraffin]

9.   Keeping records of everything including logging all train times etc.

10   Collecting tickets from passengers.

11   They were even expected to refill the Nestle's penny chocolate machine.

12.   Operating the road gates from the signal box.

13.   Loading and unloading milk churns of which there were always plenty, and parcels from the guard's van.

14.   In the summer, servicing green and cream 'camping coaches'.

That multitude of tasks was to be carried out during a 48 hour week of two shifts, 2 am till 2 pm and 2 pm to 10 pm. all for less than £3 per week.

Many scores of local grammar school pupils used the branch line to travel to various schools in the Dale. Boy and girl pupils living at Jervaulx and Leyburn travelled to the Yorkshire Grammar School at Askrigg, but they were strictly segregated into four separated carriages. The pupils who lived in villages such as East Witton Middleham and Spennithorne would cycle into the station [in all weathers] and park their bicycles in a specially built hut just behind the 'down' platform. Yorebridge Grammar School pupils were issued with a green annual railway pass by the North Riding Education Committee which for me was valid between Leyburn to Askrigg on any day. I often used the pass on a Saturday when visiting relatives in Hawes, having only to pay for the single stage between Askrigg and Hawes. Not only did I get the green annual pass, as part of a railway family, I was allowed privilege tickets at about a quarter of the normal price. For a child this amounted to 1/8th of the normal return price which was about one shilling. I handed penny ha'penny out of the window to the booking clerk who handed me the ticket where I was sitting.

During the war, ammunition trains travelled up the branch all the way to Garsdale then transferred onto the Carlisle line en route to Stranraer. The ammunition trains always travelled by night and were extremely heavy and usually headed by two locos at the front and one pushing from the rear. There was once a bit of a panic when one of the axles of a wagon began to overheat due to the lack of grease and the wagon was quickly released and shunted into a siding to allow it to cool off.

Hawes 1926. 'Pasty' Mason is left front, Joe Foster is right front and his son George Foster is lying down on the engine's running plate.

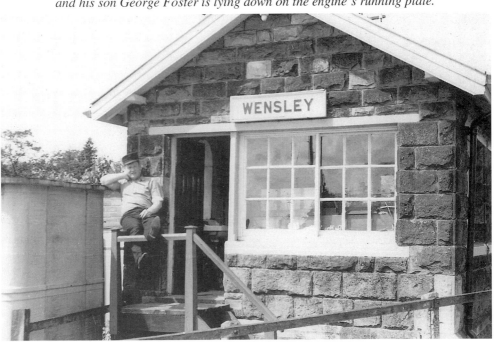

Harry Appleby relaxing outside the Wensley signal box.

The Schoolboy

Eric Walker.

 I am grateful to Eric Walker of Wellington New Zealand for his permission to use his memories in No 28 Relay magazine.

I come from a railway family with myself, father, [Reg] grandfather, [Johnny Walker] two great grandfathers [Pearson Walker and George Richardson] and great-great grandfather, [Henry Walker] on my father's side all having worked on the railways in England. I was five years old in 1938 when I went to live at Crakehall Station when my father was in charge there. I think the reason we went to live there was because my father's grandfather on his mother's side [George Richardson] had for many years been a guard at Leyburn. My father would often travel the branch line to visit him at Leyburn.

I remember as a small boy watching the many trains that stopped or passed through Crakehall station. I can recall the period during the war quite clearly. The line was open for 24 hours a day, 7 days a week, so that trains of munitions could pass on their way to the Glasgow docks. From Bedale trains were double headed. In those days there were no route availability restrictions for locomotives so the branch saw all types of locomotives. Those large driving wheels always seemed to struggle and never came to grips with the gradient. The story goes that one day while speaking to an inspector my father suggested that one engine be placed at the rear of the munitions trains instead of the front. This was done. From then on I used to stand and count the number of wagons up at the rear. If a big engine was at the rear, very rarely were more than 5 or 6 wagons buffered up, so big engines were never really suitable for the branch. It was a different matter with troop trains on which often a V2 was used. The limestone trains were worked by the Middlesbrough shed. These were hauled by J26, J39 and Q5 [they were marked with chevrons that indicated they had been in France in the First World War] and Ivatt 4s.

I also recall during the war when my father was on holiday, we went away for the day on the morning that the Teesside limestone train ran away between Jervaulx Station and Bedale. The driver gave the appropriate whistle but the temporary person on duty at Crakehall was not aware what it meant. The Bedale pickup at the time was coming out of the Esso sidings just across the points. Its engine, a J25 was hit on the cab side, peeling it back. The stone train engine J26 434, was thrown against the signal cabin. The stone train trips were a bonus turn [i.e. piece work] so, though brakes were supposed to be pinned down from Redmire and lifted at Bedale, the crews often did not do this and on several occasions trains would run past the outer home signal at danger at Bedale.

From 1944-49, I attended Northallerton Grammar School, travelling there on the train. During the bad winter of 1947 I recall that sometimes we were sent home early because of bad weather. Occasionally we were late for school due to the railway's 'steam raiser' sleeping in. On some of these occasions the engine of the limestone train was used.

Being a freight engine the manual brakes in the guards van were used to assist stopping the trains at stations. After leaving school, I started work on the railway at Leeming Bar. There I enjoyed helping to shunt the local goods and weighing the wagons of stone from Wensley for Sheffield. After doing my national service I returned to work at Bedale until the passenger trains ceased, after which I went to work at York in District Control, but that is another story.

A series of photographs taken by Eric Walker.

Eric wearing the Northallerton Grammar School cap with his father William Redvers Walker on the lever frame at Crakehall station. 1945

Eric Walker's mother Jean standing on the milk loading bay at Crakehall.

The Bedale to Northallerton with guard Fred Sharpe climbing aboard and Fred Atkinson on platform.

The last train on the 24th April 1954 pulling into Crakehall.

Lou Dale.

In the 1930s Leeming Bar station was at the peak of its efficiency as a goods and passenger station and as mentioned earlier it was at the hub of a veritable enterprise of minor industries and had a potential passenger cliental far beyond its immediate populace. A young Lou Dale became friendly with all members of the staff and was on speaking terms with every station master until the retirement of Mr. Yardley. Mr. Rowe was the Station Master just before the war and Billy Banks the chief clerk and Tom Grasby, Ernie Guest as porter/signalmen with Bill Harrison and Bill Dunne as the drivers. His favourite staff member though was Harold Gaythorpe of the signal cabin. Harold would often invite Lou and his pals to walk with him to Ham Hall, the nearest gate crossing, when he was due to renew the paraffin lamps in the signals there. Lou recalls that once after a particularly cold spell, the signal arm dropped, revealing a green light which was a potential danger. The system was changed for the arm to go up to show a green so that if it did drop, a red would show thus making it safe.

As was the norm, the incumbent station master had a domestic 'coal for sale' franchise and in the days of Station Master Rowe, Lou's father was employed to bag the coal and was paid 2d per cwt. Lou was roped in to help his father and his task was to hold the bag while his father filled it. Apparently between them they could bag five tons of coal after tea when young Lou would receive just 6d and get very dirty for his efforts into the bargain, while his dad repaired to the local pub with the rest of the money. Another extra job that his father used to do was to draw and clean the bitumen boiler used to prepare the asphalt for the runways at Leeming aerodrome, only for this job he received fire wood made from the tar barrels. This surely was an indication of the hard times faced by such families in the 1930s.

Lou remembers those days with a smile and a twinkle of his eye when both he and his pals, with a small bevy of coerced village lasses had fun and played some illegal games in and around the station and the line. They took to discovering what was in the warehouses and other buildings on the station by creeping or sneaking into them whenever the chance came. Once inside they would play cards or at times played 'Truth-Dare or Consequences' with the girls. However, he does not reveal what the 'consequences' after the dares were? The pivotal crane in the sidings was another derring-do source of fun for them, but on reflection Lou thinks that it was quite dangerous them swinging around on the crane's hook and climbing to the top of the cranes arm. It was probably as much to do with impressing the girls as anything.

RAF Leeming was a target for the Luftwaffe and Lou remembers when a Heinkel 111 flew over the station where the 'up' and the 'down' train were both in the station letting off steam. Most of the villagers came out to watch as they had heard the drone of the bomber's engines as it approached but at the last moment it turned and dived to strafe the aerodrome. [The attack was from the east and one of the hangar doors was holed in several places and the holes were still visible until the door was refurbished in the early 1980s]. It is believed that the Heinkel was eventually shot down by a Spitfire from Catterick.

The Vale of Mowbray bacon factory was the largest concern for the station in terms of regular business. On most late afternoons, wagon loads of pigs and cattle were brought into the station and Lou and his pals would help to usher them into the factory, blithely unaware of the fate awaiting those bewildered animals. Brood mares would arrive at the station for transporting to the Theakston Stud some five miles from Leeming Bar.

In 1938 the Bomber Command aerodrome at Leeming was being constructed and huge amounts of materiel for the contractors arrived by goods trains on a regular basis until the station became officially operational in 1940.The construction work on the drome was ongoing due to the continual upgrading and changing role of the air field.

The first station master that Lou got to know was Mr. Rowe followed by Mr. Hill then Mr. Yardley the last master of the station before its final closure. Lou Dale who stills lives in the village of Leeming Bar became friendly with all the station staff as they came and went and he is a direct link for many of the memories of the busiest LNER station on the Wensleydale line.

A consignment of second hand tractors for John Henry Gill Farm Implements arriving at Leeming Bar in 1945.L to R J.A. Gill, Mr. How, William Gill, Frank Gill, John Henry Gill. The small boy is the current sales director Malcolm Gill.

Accidents!

Accidents and collisions on railways have been part and parcel of the industry ever since its introduction in the nineteenth century. In the early days there were many accidents due to what might be called the birth pangs due to the learning of the network coupled with the 'railway mania' that enveloped the country with the arrival of the industrial revolution. As inexperience gave way to expertise and skill, the number of accidents diminished, but rail accidents will never be a thing of the past.

It wasn't only the larger mainline rail companies that had accidents, the small inconsequential lines had their share of calamity, and the Wensleydale line was no exception. Research among the archive of contemporary newspapers and associated journals reveals that there have been several accidents of varying severity on the branch line in the past hundred or so years.

Bedale.

In December 1901 there was an accident at Bedale station which caused the death of the fireman of a 'Bogie Tank' Passenger engine No. 465. There had been a bout of severe wet weather and flood water undermined a section of the line approaching the station. The subsidence caused the locomotive to overturn, trapping the unfortunate fireman when the engine slid down the embankment and landed on its side. This made the recovery work an extremely awkward and complicated operation. The recovery engineers rigged up a block and tackle system and utilised three locomotives to haul the recalcitrant tank engine out of its embedded position. An 'A' class locomotive acted as 'sheet anchor' while the other two engines edged away in opposite directions. Slowly but surely the derailed engine was hauled upright allowing the recovery of the unfortunate fireman. The bogie engine was sent for repair and was back on the line in a very short time.

Garsdale

The most serious accident to occur on the line happened on the 24th December 1910. Garsdale to Hawes line was in fact part of the Midland Railway and as such, locomotives from other parts of the country operated on that stretch. On that night there were no fewer that nine light engines in and around the station. Two of those engines were MR class No 448 and No. 548 driven respectively by Edwin Scott and George Bath. Both drivers were keen to travel back to Carlisle, [it was Christmas Eve] and a mood of 'rushing to get the job done' was in the air. They were both kept waiting on the sidings by signalman Alfred Sutton. Both drivers failed to carry out 'Rule 55' which stated that when a train was detained on a running line, the guard, fireman or shunter, should go to the signal box to remind the signalman of the position of the train'.

Signalman Sutton under increasing pressure, tried to find [rail] paths for a number of 'up' and 'down' trains. Overwhelmed by the volume of those nine engines and fatigue brought on by an ongoing ten hour shift, he decided to accept an 'up' express. In the meantime the two Carlisle engines had been shunted onto the 'down' mainline. Signalman Sutton then changed the starting signals from red to green, and the two Carlisle engine drivers assumed that it was the signal for them to proceed to their destinations and set off into the murk of the night. Three minutes later the 'double headed' Scotch Express thundered through the station all the time gaining on the two Carlisle trains. The express driver through the gloom saw the red tail lights of loco No. 548 and applied the brakes while at the same time George Bath driving the rear most loco, increased his speed to try to reduce any impact between the two trains. Without doubt his actions helped to reduce the coming impact, but in the event both engines on the express were de-railed as was one of the light engines. The impact came just north of the Moorcock Tunnel and as a result the two leading carriages telescoped and escaping Pintsch gas ignited causing a conflagration. All those at the scene made desperate efforts to rescue the passengers but twelve people died, including a five month old baby. Signalman Sutton on surveying the scene was struck speechless and went into what would be now described as deep shock. Although he may have been responsible for those unfolding events, one must sympathise with him and the onerous tasks he faced with so much traffic in such a short space of time. The baby girl that died in the crash lies buried in the churchyard at Hawes.

Less than three years later tragedy and disaster struck Garsdale once again. A combination of overload, poor quality coal and it must be said, negligence by those involved was responsible for the ensuing accident.

Deely locomotive No 993 was heading the express from Carlisle to St. Pancras originating from Glasgow. This train was extremely heavy with nine carriages and weighing close on 250 tons and under other circumstances should have been double headed. The solo 993 locomotive struggled to draw its heavy load over Ais Gill summit but to no avail. To add to the problem of overload, the tender had been filled with low grade 'slack' and as valiantly as the fireman tried to keep the pressure up, the engine could not maintain sufficient steam, coming to a standstill a couple of miles from the actual summit. The rules at the time were that if a train was stalled on a stretch of line the crew was to protect their train by the placing of detonators. This, the crew failed to do. The crew of a following train failed to reduce speed and also failed to notice the frantic hand signals of the signalman at Mallerstang. As a result the speeding train ran into the rear of the stalled express smashing its way through two coaches. Escaping gas ignited causing the wrecked coaches to catch fire which engulfed the entire scene. Fourteen people were killed in the accident once again caused by human error. Garsdale was earning a reputation as a jinxed station.

Crakehall

One tragic event which without doubt was an accident in the truest sense of the word occurred at Crakehall station on the 23rd September 1915. During the safety carriage door checks prior to a train's departure, the Station Master Mr. Gregory Potter hurried along the platform to close a carriage door that he had spotted being slightly ajar. Unfortunately as he hurried along the platform to close the door, he bumped into a porter carrying out similar checks, both were walking backwards. The impact threw Mr. Potter under the rails of the train wheels which caused him multiple injuries. He was taken to the Rutson

Hospital in Northallerton as quickly as was possible, but died of his injuries the following day.

Jervaulx

A tragic accident occurred one evening in 1953 between Leyburn and Jervaulx for which the railway authorities could not be blamed and involved just one man and the last train from Hawes. Local farm worker John Horner was heading home after attending a musical evening at the village of Newton le Willows. John played the concertina in a harmonic band with a group of friends and after the evening's entertainment had ended, he set off for home. The walk was no great distance and he always walked on the road so as to avoid the rail track until he had to cross it to get to where he lived but always knowing that the last train of the day had passed. The night in question was very wild and windy with the wind causing the trees to gush and rustle. It was also quite cool and with head down jacket collar pulled up high John strode onto the line safe in the knowledge that there were no more trains. He walked down the track and into the howling wind but, unbeknown to John, the last train from Hawes had been delayed and as he walked he was completely unaware of its approach, as were the driver and the fireman unaware of John on the track. John was killed instantly within a few yards of where he would have stepped off the line to his home. This tragedy was all due to a set of circumstances which on their own were trivial, but combined proved to be lethal.

Yafforth Gates

Another heart breaking accident occurred in March 1958 that involved Mrs. Irene Williams, Crossing Keeper at Yafforth Gates, the first crossing on the down line from Northallerton.

I am very grateful to Mrs. Carlton, the daughter of Mrs. Williams, for giving me her full permission to relate the events of this particularly sad story.

On March 6th 1958 a racehorse train tender left Northallerton station bound for Leyburn to collect a number of racehorses from the stables of Middleham and slowly steamed toward the gates at Yafforth. The board signals were against the train as Mrs. Williams came out of the house at 6.20 am to close the gates to road traffic. For some unknown reason, the driver of the engine did not respond to the signal and in the early morning fog came straight on over the crossing. While attempting to close the gates, Mrs. Williams was struck by the engine and killed instantly. The engine driver carried on with his journey totally unaware of the accident and that one of the crossing gates was attached to the buffers of his tender. By this time a frantic and horror stricken Mr. Williams had telephoned Ainderby station, the next stop along the line, and informed a stunned Station Master, Mr. Lynn of the dreadful accident.

There was the usual enquiry and inquest but there were no recriminations held against the crew of the train who were deeply shocked and traumatised by this completely avoidable human tragedy.

Not only did Mr. Williams lose his wife, the family of eight children lost their mother.

Close run occurrences

Garsdale
On the 17th October 1917, fire gutted the road engine shed on the 'up' side of the lines. There were no casualties but an engine had to be sent to Darlington for a total refit. Then there was the oft told story of the engine being turned round on the turntable at Garsdale Junction when a strong and gusting wind, not an unknown foe in that part of the world, took control of the whole operation and the locomotive and table span round and round on its axis. The 'table' was brought to a halt by the frantic shovelling of stones and cinders into the pit to slow it down. To prevent any recurrence of the wind problem, a skirt of timber was eventually thrown around the turntable in the form a stockade. This not only solved the problem of high winds, it also protected it from drifting snow.

Northallerton
A potential accident was prevented in 1913 by quick thinking of the staff at Northallerton. Engine BTP No. 324 had been cleared by signal to the 'up' platform when one member of the staff, [a driver] realised that the next 'up' express was approaching against its signals. The driver climbed aboard the BPT and set it in motion and then quickly clambered out. This action gave the driver of the express enough time to realise what was happening and stop his train. The BPT carried on heading south but was finally brought to a halt on the outskirts of Thirsk.

Bedale
In 1988 an ore/dust train returning from Redmire was trundling through Bedale crossing and as the middle section reached the crossing, several of the dust hoppers left the line as rotting sleepers collapsed. The over turning hoppers then ruptured the rails and brought the whole train and station to a halt. The accident caused a delay that severely affected the passing road traffic to and from Bedale and happened very close to the petrol depot at nearby Aiskew. Harry Appleby was the duty signalman on that day and he happened to be standing at the bottom of the steps of the signal box holding the signal tablet for collection when the accident began to unfold. Harry made a rapid and less than dignified retreat as hoppers began to overturn. He said later that if the train had been travelling in the opposite direction he almost certainly would have been hit by a hopper and the signal box would have been demolished. Due to the slow speed of the train the only damage was to the rails and the sleepers, with a section of fencing turned into matchwood. Although it was classed as a minor accident, it took more than forty eight hours to clear the debris and for the line to be back in operation.

Harmby Quarry level crossing.
I am indebted to Irene Bradley for the following information about her late father and an incident at the Harmby level crossing. There follows a draft of the reports in two newspapers.

The People from our own correspondent Leyburn. Yorks Saturday.

Jumped for life when engine stalled on level crossing.
[Saturday 6th September 1936]

Mr. Mawer Hammond a director of the Leyburn Stone and Macadam Co. Ltd had a narrow escape from death today when his motor car was wrecked by a passenger train from Northallerton at the Harmby Quarry crossing.

Mr. Hammond was leaving the quarry. When he reached the main line metals, the engine of his car stalled. The train was then not twenty yards away. Mr. Hammond was just able to leap from the car before it was struck by the locomotive and wrecked.

There was a second report in the Sunday Graphic.

Jumped to live.
[7th September 1936]

Man's car stalled on railway line, hit by engine. Twenty yards away was a train bearing down on the car. He leapt just as the engine struck the car and escaped death.

That was the experience of Mr. Mawer Hammond of Leyburn Yorkshire, a director of the Leyburn Stone and Macadam Co. Ltd at Harmby Quarry level crossing yesterday. Mr. Hammond was leaving the quarry. The train was signalled but not yet in sight. When he reached the main line metals the engine of his car stalled.

There were reports also in The News of the World, The Sunday Dispatch and two local issues.

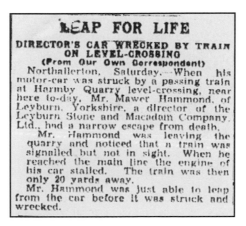

A contemporary newspaper cutting of the event.

Black Saturday
24th April 1954

Although the date for the closure is always recognised as the 24th of April, the official notice by British Railways announcing the closure of passenger services on the Wensleydale line was for Monday 26th of April. The closing of the Northallerton-Garsdale railway line and many other branch lines around the country was inevitable, as the increase in other forms of transport chiefly the ownership of the private car which was the dream and then the reality of the travelling public. The population of the Dale served by the line had been in steady decline for a number of years as the movement of people to the urban areas increased. It became apparent that the losses the line was incurring [£14,500 per annum] could not be sustained and in 1953 closure or part closure was deemed to be the answer. Quite naturally the Dales folk protested most strongly and meetings were held between the North Eastern Transport User's Committee and British Rail. It was all to no avail and closure was fixed for the 29th of March 1954. This date was not acceptable as an alternative bus service being provided was not ready due to a delay in licensing problems. When the closure came it was a partial affair with a passenger service maintained between Garsdale and Hawes, but Crakehall and Finghall Lane station were to be closed forthwith. However, Ainderby, Scruton, Leeming Bar, Bedale, Jervaulx, Constable Burton, Spennithorne, Leyburn, Wensley, Redmire, Aysgarth and Askrigg would remain open for goods and parcel traffic. The crucial service [in the eyes of the Dales folk] was the loss of the passenger service from Northallerton. The User's Committee kept up the protest but British Transport Commission was adamant and the date for the closure was set for the 26th April 1954, which was to be the actual day that the service stopped as opposed to the last day that the service would run. The last passenger train between Northallerton, Hawes and Garsdale was the 4.10pm on Saturday the 24th April and the train was to be pulled by a J21 class 65038 an engine built in 1889. The usual and much younger 673435 Tank engine [built 1901] was relegated to shunting work in the station as it was considered to be unsuitable for this last journey as four carriages were required to take the number of passengers clamouring to travel on it. A British Rail official stated, with no little irony, that as far as the Transport Commission was concerned it was a day for rejoicing, as £14,500 per annum would be saved and if the people of the Dales had patronised the service as they were doing so on its final run, there would have been no need to close it in the first place. As cold and unfeeling as that statement seemed, it was the stark truth.

Came the day and although the last official passenger train ran on the 24th April 1954, the service went out in style and not without a little black humour. This is how the occasion was reported in the local newspaper, the Northern Echo which bore the headline;

BLACK FOR THE LAST TRAIN.

Wensleydale turned out in force on Saturday evening to pay its last respects to '*Old Faithful*' the train which since the Northallerton-Garsdale line was opened in 1878, has regularly made the journey between the two stations. The 4.10pm train on Saturday was the last passenger train to make the full journey and return. The line is now closed but for parcel and freight traffic.

A funereal atmosphere was created by black ribbons tied to the back of the train and by laying of a laurel wreath on the front lamp of the engine by the incumbent Rector of Bolton-cum-Redmire the Reverend D.T. Reynolds-Carling. Also the appearance of Mr. Jeff Pocklington, undertaker of Crakehall who stood on the platform in tail coat and pin stripe trousers, with his black hat held respectfully in his hand, which he donned then doffed with a sweeping gesture as the train departed, added to the sombre moment of the day.

Sombre moment it may have been, but the ensuing throng treated the occasion more as a holiday. The four passenger coaches, three more than usual all filled up well in Northallerton. The passengers were railway historians, Wensleydale folk making a last sentimental journey and a few people who were going home after a days shopping at Northallerton plus a collection of former employees which included, Mr. William Shannon, booking clerk at Aysgarth, Jim Almond a former goods porter and Herbert Newson, a former driver who had all begun their railway careers on the line. The oldest passenger was Mrs. Frances Palmer whose husband was an earlier stationmaster at Jervaulx and whose son was the current station master there. The youngest passenger was Robert Lambert of Aysgarth whose mother took him on the trip as her father had travelled on the very first train when the line opened, so it seemed only right that his great-grandson should be on the last. Mrs. Margaret Horner aged 85 of Swininthwaite was booked on the train as she had witnessed the first gaily decorated train run through when the final stretch of line was opened between Askrigg and Hawes in 1878.

At various stations en route to Garsdale there were small crowds and it was not until the return journey particularly between Garsdale and Leyburn that the real crowds turned up. They came in force to say farewell to 'Old Faithful' on her last journey and to cheer the driver Ronald May of Northallerton, fireman Derick Appleton of Thirsk and the guard George Ezzard of Morton on Swale, the crew whose destiny it was to take the last passenger train to run on the Wensleydale line from Northallerton to Hawes. On arriving at Ainderby Steeple a Union Jack flew at half mast and the vicar, the Rev. F. Lishman and Mrs. Lishman were on the platform to see the train off, but at Scruton and Leeming Bar there were very few passengers for the train. At Bedale there was a large crowd, including many children and then the train steamed on through to Crakehall and Finghall, the two stations which were already closed. At Constable Burton there was a long halt as the down train from Garsdale bearing the chalked inscription 'No Sympathy Wanted' swept past. At Spennithorne the route began to traverse some of Wensleydale's most beautiful countryside with Pen Hill and Coverdale in the far distance glowering beneath heavy skies pierced here and there by shafts of sunlight.

Derick Appleton the fireman on that last train recalls that day from a different perspective. For Ronald May, George Ezzard and Derick it was just another passenger run. Those who did not know him might have been forgiven for thinking that he had dressed up especially for the occasion as he was wearing a clean shirt, collar and tie, but then Derick always did wear a clean shirt, collar and tie. Even when the going was hot and sweaty stoking the fire, he refused to even so much as undo his tie and to this day is a collar and tie man. The other two members of the crew were also wearing a collar and tie on that day, but for that day alone. On that last run Derick sweated more than usual. After firing the little tank engine on a regular basis, Derick found that he had to 'pepper' the new engine with coal to keep up a good head of steam with having those four carriages in tow. Quite a thirst could be worked up shovelling the coal and the 'elbow benders' in the special carriage offered Ronnie and Derick a crate of ale to slake their thirsts, but they had to refuse as it was strictly against the rules. At the end of the day's proceedings, Derick signed off and made a swift getaway toward the platform where the train heading for Thirsk stood and went straight home. When the line closed completely in 1963, he was

Fireman Derick Appleton receiving the wreath from The Reverend Reynolds-Carling to be placed on the lamp holder of 'Old Faithful'

offered a job at Blythe in Northumberland, but after much thought, declined and left the railway for good.

Although that run on the 24th was the last full service, the following day, the evening 'up' milk train from Leyburn to Northallerton was the last train to carry passengers. As that G5 class engine No 67345 puffed its way into Northallerton station at 6 o' clock that evening, it signalled the final ending of passenger services on the Wensleydale railway line.

With the ending of the passenger service, there was an almost inevitability that the goods and parcel service would go the same way. Indeed, Crakehall and Finghall Lane had lost their goods service on the same day as they lost the passenger service. On the 3rd of July 1967 Wensley was the last station on the route to lose its goods and parcels service, the other stations succumbing to the power of economics and British Rail in the intervening years from April 1954. However, there was a beacon of hope for the line when Leyburn and Redmire escaped the axe as those two stations were left open for the running of limestone trains albeit on an irregular basis. Although closure was what it meant, it will be noted that Jervaulx still carried school passengers to Aysgarth School after the general withdrawal of regular traffic. This was due to the importance of the school as being one of the leading Preparatory schools in the country and could still provide a viable and constant passenger list.

Along with the geographical oddity of Jervaulx station being actually in Newton le Willows, likewise was Aysgarth School. The change of station name came about when Lord Aylesbury, the owner of the adjacent Jervaulx estate, had the railway authorities change the station name from Newton le Willows to Jervaulx when he discovered that many of his invited guests were finding themselves stranded at Newton le Willows in Lancashire.

The original Aysgarth School first opened in Richmond, moved for a single term to Saltburn-by-the-Sea, finally settling its location and nationwide success in Newton le Willows [Yorkshire] where to this day despite a devastating fire in 1933 it is still a thriving education establishment.

Alyn Armstrong, who was a porter/signalman at Jervaulx station in the early 1950s, recalls that when the school summer holidays commenced, the scholars who prided themselves on being called 'Aysgarthians' would board the train known endearingly as the 'Jervaulx Express' for the first part of their journey home. One of the many tasks asked of Alyn was to carry and barrow dozens of luggage trunks and boxes belonging to the scholars, many marked 'Not wanted on voyage' onto the train's luggage van. Their destinations like that of the scholars were far and wide to their parents' homes, situated in such exotic locations as Cape Town, Salisbury, Rio de Janeiro and Buenos Aires. On the return of the schoolboys, the shifting and lifting of the luggage was carried out once again

The final closure of the line caused a stir amongst enthusiasts and non enthusiasts far and wide. In an effort to forestall the dreaded day, Dales Tours were organised and interested associations and individuals filled three passenger specials in the dying days of 1992. The very last train was a diesel driven train consisting of thirteen coaches bearing the rather sad

The 4.10 ready for the flag at Northallerton. George Ezzard, Derick Appleton, Ronald May Schoolboy unknown.

Derick Appleton through the 'starboard window' of Old Faithful.

Derick Appleton and Jim May look out of the cab of the last official passenger train from Northallerton as it approaches Garsdale.

name of 'Wensleydale Lament'. On January 2nd 1993 the train left King's Cross Station at 7.40am arriving at Redmire at 1.30pm. Forthwith British Rail put the line which was valued at £1.1 million pounds up for sale and invited bids, although still having overall control. That is when the Wensleydale Railway Association stepped in and the rescue act for the line began its arduous and somewhat fretful journey to once again being a vibrant and viable railway line.

Posters from the Past

The official notice informing the public of the closure of passenger services on the entire Wensleydale line.

The end of the line for passenger services at Wensley.

The Wensleydale
Railway Association.

The Wensleydale Railway Association is a thriving organisation with a membership well in excess of 3,000 which includes enthusiasts as far away as Australia and the United States. This huge membership has been achieved by the dedication and sheer hard work of a body of people campaigning for the reinstatement of the line.

In 1990 Ruth Annison and Scott Handley, along with similar interested parties, got together to investigate the feasibility of re-establishing the rail link between Northallerton and Garsdale. The result was the forming of the Wensleydale Railway Association on the 23rd of May that same year. It was to be a daunting task. Much of the track had been lifted after its closure, with only 22 miles remaining between Northallerton and Redmire. The purpose of the WRA was to reinvigorate the branch line to something like its previous status and incorporate it into a public transport system with a view to running passenger services and eventually re-build the 18 miles 'missing link' between Redmire and Garsdale. It was also envisaged that there might be day trips with the use of heritage trains pulled by heritage engines both steam and diesel for nostalgia trips. However, the overall aim planned by the Association was, and is, to run a modern efficient railway. While these ideas were being pursued, there was still a regular run of stone carrying trains from Redmire to Redcar which kept British Rail interested in the line. However an unexpected problem arose when British Steel decided to have the stone ferried by road. A lengthy and vigorous 'Rail not Road' campaign by all interested parties to keep the stone transported by rail, [not least because of the potential damage to the local roads by fleets of lorries] resulted in British Steel opting to utilise the stone quarried at Shap in Cumbria. In the midst of the campaign British Steel closed its Ravenscraig plant. This was an enormous set back for the WRA as it meant that the entire line would be totally unused as British Rail announced its closure. To its credit, the Association and its members did not flinch and pressed ahead with plans to purchase the line which had been valued by an independent source of being half the valuation of £1.1 million pounds that had been published by British Rail. In March 1993 a campaign was launched to raise the necessary funds through donations of 'track units' at £15 per unit. Then came another twist in the saga. British Rail announced it was withdrawing the line from offer of sale. The reason? The section of line between Northallerton and Redmire was to be utilised by the MoD for the transporting of armoured fighting vehicles between Salisbury Plain and Catterick Garrison. The MoD invested £750,000 for upgrading of that section of line to be utilised. The publicity generated by the involvement of the MoD helped the rapid expansion of the WRA. By

June the Track Unit Fund had raised more than £100,000.

The high capital cost for revamping the 18 miles missing link was estimated by British Rail to be £1m per running mile. The raising of the necessary funds was by far the greatest hurdle that confronted the WRA committee, but they set about raising the money with great enthusiasm and a great deal of fiscal logic. This was helped in 2000 by the forming of Wensleydale Railway plc and the issuing of a Share Offers and a separate Wensleydale Railway Trust Ltd. for charitable purposes.

A subsidiary company, Wensleydale Railway [Properties] Ltd now owns Aysgarth station and rents part as a holiday cottage. It also owns Leeming Bar station and has Leyburn station under lease, each having a thriving shop replete with all things railwayana. Leeming Bar station has on site, ready to use diesel locomotives and multiple units, a complete works train including a diesel rail crane and a Bedford Bruff road/rail vehicle, several types of rolling stock, a fully functioning buffet car and 'Pilgrim', a narrow gauge steam railway. In 2001 Railtrack donated to the Trust, a mile of track from the Settle-Carlisle line which had become redundant. Beginning in July regular runs from Leeming Bar to Leyburn will begin, which hopefully will lead to a scheduled service as part of a transport system in its own right. Beginning in July 2003, runs between Leeming Bar and Leyburn will develop into regular rail service.

The Association is thriving and membership is growing. The quarterly magazine 'Relay' that arrives promptly on the door mats of the homes of all members, is of the highest quality and is chock full of information and photographs of all things railway. The Patrons of The WRA are, the distinguished actor Robert Hardy CBE, The Lord Bolton, the entertainer Mike Harding, TV personality Michael Palin and Christopher Awdry son of the Rev. Awdry, creator of Thomas the Tank Engine. The late and great 'Honorary Yorkshireman' Bill Owen of "Last of the Summer Wine" fame was a previous Patron and to his final days was very supportive of the whole enterprise.

With the continued enthusiasm and sheer hard work being put in by all the members and the committee, the WR can only go from strength to strength.

The Wensleydale Railway can be found on the World Wide Web at; HYPERLINK "http://WWW.Wensleydalerailway.com" www.wensleydalerailway.com .

A Gallery

of

Wensleydale

Railway

Characters

Don Allen
Signalman

Alyn Armstrong
Porter/Signalman

Bill Archer
Signalman

Artie Rainbow Jr
Platelayer

John Braithwaite
Platelayer

Lanny Cass
Signalman

James Blades
Signalman

George Catchpole
Engine driver

Bill Catchpole
Wagonman

Jack Castle
Guard

Artie Rainbow Snr
Platelayer

Laurie Atkinson
Engine driver

George Catchpole
Engine driver

Norman Darby
Station Master

Jack Dent
Road motor fitter

Tony Eaton
Motor driver

George Foster
Porter

Harold Gaythorpe
Signalman

Derek Fawcett
Rolling stock
technician

Harry Hartley
Trackwalker

John Hatch
Guard

Jack Heseltine
Motor driver

Alan Hiscock
Signalman

Eric Irving
Signalman

Ursula Jackson
Porter

Herbert Jobling
Motor driver
/Signalman

Edgar Martin
Fireman

Chris Megginson
Engine driver

Joyce Merryweather
Clerk

Nessfield Hartley
Signalman

George Parsley
Trackwalker

Dick Pashby Snr
Engine driver

Dick Pashby Jnr
Telegraph worker

Mr. Pearson
Inspector

Tom Plummer
Station Master

Bill Redhead
Crossing keeper

Derick Dunning
Fireman

Fred Stevens
Trackwalker

Ann Stubbs
Clerk

Alan Surtees
Engine driver

George Walls
Station Master

Sidney Weighell
NUR
General Secretary

Maurice Weighell
Engine driver

Tommy Weighell
Signalman

Arthur Yardley
Station Master

Arthur Severs
Lad Porter

Ken Brown
Fireman

Will Hatfield
Engine driver

Fred Severs
Guard

Stan Hatfield
Fireman

Wilf Robinson
Guard

Couples

Kathleen and Alan Gaythorpe
Clerk and engine driver

Sue and Bob Appleby
Crossing keeper and signalman

Mr and Mrs Williams
Crossing keepers

Wilf and Sheila Houseman
Signalman and Clerk

Eric Walker -Jean Walker -Reg Walker
Clerk-   Crossing Keeper-Leading Porter

Rear cover pictures. 'Old Faithful' being garlanded with the farewell wreath. [Appleton]
The station staff at Hawes 1946. [Irving] A team of trackmen 1930 [Shuttleworth]